Commentland

A Decade of
UK Comment & Opinion
2009–2019

An Editorial Intelligence Report
editorialintelligence.com

With thanks to: Alice Feilden, Karen Persad and Laura Musins from the Editorial Intelligence team, with research help from Adam Solomons. And to Julia Koppitz and John Bond at whitefox. Cover design by Hayden Brown and Theo Borgvin Weiss. A special thanks to Barclays, Virgin Media and Edwardian Hotels for their support in the publication of this book. *Commentland* was conceived and created by Julia Hobsbawm.

First published in 2019 by
Editorial Intelligence

editorialintelligence.com

Copyright © Editorial Intelligence, 2019

The authors assert their moral right to be identified as the authors of this work.

All rights reserved. No part of this publication may be reproduced, stored in a retrieval system or transmitted in any form or by any means, electronic, mechanical, photocopying, recording or otherwise, without prior written permission of the authors.

While every effort has been made to trace the owners of copyright material reproduced herein, the authors and publishers would like to apologise for any omissions and will be pleased to incorporate missing acknowledgments in any future editions.

ISBN 978-0-95-591035-7

Project management by whitefox
Designed and typeset by seagulls.net
Cover design by Hayden Brown and Theo Borgvin Weiss
Printed and bound in Great Britain by Clays Ltd, Elcograf S.p.A

Contents

Editor's Note – *Sophie Radice*	1
The best commentary rings like a bell – *Stephen Fleming*	3
When anonymity breeds kindness – *Justine Roberts*	6
The intolerable intolerance of the intolerant – *Dylan Jones*	9
Freedom of speech vs licence to offend – *Yasmin Alibhai-Brown*	12
Policy can change the inequalities gap – *Adrian Monck*	15
My unspun heroes – *Anthony Seldon*	18
Why a real diversity of opinion is essential to the survival of comment – *Claire Fox*	21
Can we heal our divided country? – *Deborah Mattinson*	25
It's the climate, stupid – *Ed Gillespie*	28
Comment is the skeleton key to understanding – *Geraldine Sharpe-Newton*	32
The bitter and shallow battles of the Brexit debate – *Gisela Stuart*	36
Lucky me – *Jane Brien*	39
The comment bull and bear market – *Julia Hobsbawm*	42

Money and freedom – *Matt Peacock*   45

Why Meghan Markle shouldn't wear nude tights   49
– *Rachel Johnson*

Sacred fact, profane data – *Sanjay Nazerali*   52

A view from below – *Solomon Elliott*   55

Sex and comment – *Stephanie Theobald*   60

The commentators' journey towards Brexit – *Peter Morgan*   64

Why the UK media failed to see the crash was coming   67
– *Vicky Pryce*

Quicker, smarter but still out of touch – *Stephanie Flanders*   71

Interview with Yanis Varoufakis – *Julia Hobsbawm*   74

Contributor biographies   81

Comment Awards: Winners 2009–2018   89

Editor's note

Sophie Radice

We asked a group of writers and thinkers to write a piece each to mark the Comment Award's tenth anniversary. Our brief was loose, allowing for an individual response. Most authors wrote about the changing landscape of comment and commentators from different angles and contexts while others responded by writing their own 'thought piece' born out of their own very personal experience. I think the variety and scope of the essays does justice to the exciting, surprising and often controversial Comment Awards.

I'm pretty sure that I've been to every Comment Award over the last decade. I've lurked around in a 'family hold back' kind of way as a long-standing member of the Editorial Intelligence team and observed the commentators and opinion makers at work/play – hopefully less creepily than that sounds.

It's not an exaggeration to say that the atmosphere of each award was a fascinating barometer of the state of comment/opinion piece journalism of the time. The first few years of awards were full of excitement because it was such a new thing for commentators to be recognised and applauded for defining the character of their publication, keeping the readers engaged and loyal to the publication's brand and informing and even amusing them in the process. It was still a world in which commuters, breakfast eaters, CEOs, political researchers and just about anyone who wanted to know what to think about something or to react against something would read their 'go-to' opinion giver, often before they had read the rest of the news.

Commentland

In the years that followed we saw the awards embrace the bloggers, the online magazines and the tweeters. Many of the commentators were forced out of any smugness and complacency (and there was definitely some) by the challenges of an ever-growing non-print readership. Some of them became bloggers, wrote for online magazines and tweeted like mad. The sensitivities of the commentators and their editors increased year by year and not only reflected a changing demographic of people reading opinions but wanting to make their opinions heard. The startlingly flouncy nature of the awards of 2018 mirrored our nervy and divided country, dominated by uncertain and temperamental Brexit politics.

Interesting times for commentary and commentators then. It's thrilling when people take a stance, and a counter-stance and even a counter-counter-stance. Otherwise things can get dull and a bit same-y. Who is giving their opinion and who is listening and responding to that opinion is changing fast and that can only be a good stagnation buster, can't it?

But that's just my opinion...

The best commentary rings like a bell

Stephen Fleming

Every morning for ten years, up until the long hot summer of 2018, I read all the comment in the UK daily press. I would then put that material into a highlights package called the 'Daily Digest' for Editorial Intelligence which was then distributed via email. The Digest was kind of like Match of the Day with me as a very poor man's Gary Lineker.

That's a lot of opinions and, mostly, the specifics of all that polemic have long left me but, like many of our memories, the general impressions remain. Some of them were pathetic, preposterous, self-serving and vain in the extreme; others were passionate, beautifully crafted and breathtakingly brilliant. My categorisations are unlikely to match those of yours.

The themes of comment vary with the news agenda. Nowadays it is difficult to think of a time when Brexit and Trump were not *the* topics of debate, but a few years ago few people were bothered by membership of the European Union or a comedic US tycoon. How times change.

And that's the thing. The subject of comment over a period reflects the things that we care about.

Over the past ten years we have cared about, and variously commented on, the Iraq War, Afghanistan, the credit crunch, coalition government, inner-city riots, climate change, the London Olympics, RBS, MPs' expenses, Scottish independence, terrorism in the UK and Syria to name but a few.

Commentland

Over that time opinion writing has become more important to us because of the accessibility and ubiquitous nature of news. Everyone knows within minutes that a general election has been called and you don't have to buy a newspaper to find that out. But you can rely on a newspaper to find out what political experts think about the fact that one *is* being held.

Comment helps us think, helps us form our opinions but can also shape those opinions. Ten years ago newspapers led the way in delivery of comment – part of a far from perfect but regulated press where bias is tolerated but accuracy is policed. Social media has ridden roughshod over that tradition and given a platform to extremism. The unsayable has become the sayable and the unthinkable is now being thought about.

Predictably, mainstream media has followed suit. The Overton window, or the window of discourse, is a term beloved of political scientists. It describes the range of policy options that are considered acceptable at a certain time. Comment has helped to shift that window and extremism has become normalised.

Consequently, comment has become increasingly polarised over the past ten years – as have we. Newspapers that once tolerated views and commissioned writers who might contradict the natural inclinations of their readership have fallen back on their core values.

Polarisation of comment, both in newspapers and online, has had a curious effect on UK politics. The mainstream parties now seem closer together in policy than perhaps ever before. A commonly held, and arguably justifiable, view among the electorate is that the parties are all the same. A discredited political class is thought to have somehow let down voters and betrayed the trust that we once had in them. In turn, policy has followed public opinion rather than led it. Knee-jerk reaction has replaced long-term strategic thinking.

Newspaper comment has fuelled this fire over the past decade. As the industry faces pressures from online media and the challenge of digital monetisation it has hedged its bets. Good business in troubled times? Maybe so, but at what cost?

Even the United Kingdom's lame duck prime minister Theresa May thinks the decline of journalism is a threat to democracy and in 2018 launched a review into the possibility of state intervention.

A report commissioned by the Department for Digital, Culture, Media and Sport found that total press advertising expenditure (excluding digital) has declined across the national and regional/local press by 70 per cent in the past 10 years, from £4.6bn in 2007 to an estimated £1.4bn in 2017. That same report noted that frontline journalists employed by news brands declined from 23,000 to 17,000 over the same period.

Democracy faces a perfect storm – a mistrust of expert commentators, the decline of the press, a mistrust of politicians, effective lobbying from mega corporations, sophisticated digital campaigning and public lethargy.

Great comment helps us think whether we agree with it or not. The best comment pieces, when you read them, ring like a bell – they are in tune with the moment. These are turbulent times and our opinions matter.

It is useful to remind ourselves of what great people think about things – that's why great comment is just that, great. Let me leave you with this piece of eighteenth-century comment from Dublin-born statesman Edmund Burke.

'When bad men combine, the good must associate; else they will fall, one by one, an unpitied sacrifice in a contemptible struggle.'

When anonymity breeds kindness

Justine Roberts

Some authors talk about the moment when their characters spring to life in the pages of a manuscript, acquiring motivations and personality, wilfully doing things their inventor had not planned. There was a distinct moment, back in the early 2000s, when I experienced something similar. Mumsnet's talk boards, previously populated by me posting under a variety of pseudonyms, suddenly began to talk among themselves. A friend of mine, after a conversation that came quite close to blackmail, had been induced to post a question about her pregnancy palpitations; instantaneously, quite miraculously, someone else – *not* me – posted an answer. A real-life Mumsnetter had entered the building, and after that things were never quite the same.

Since then, hundreds of thousands of people – most of them women – have used Mumsnet to say what they think. There are many aspects to Mumsnet Talk, but free expression and diversity of opinion is our *sine qua non*, and the one that has always set us a little bit apart.

Our society has some pretty odd ideas about mothers: they are supposed to be unstintingly generous, unfailingly kind, endlessly supportive, tirelessly devoted (to other people), and generally quite insular, humourless and thick. One of our great joys has been providing a platform that allows these women to behave like the clever, supportive, analytical, stubborn, scabrous, insightful, odd, thoughtful, informed and hilarious people they actually are. From our Academics' Corner to our World Cup topic, via Alcohol Support, Chicken-Keepers, Feminism, LGBT Parents, Miscarriage, Philosophy and Scotsnet, they give the lie over and over again to the notion that mothers confine themselves to gentle chat about nappy absorbencies.

Many of the biggest moments in the Mumsnet story make more sense when viewed through this lens of collective astonishment that mothers are fully rounded human beings. We did our first politics webchat with David Cameron (remember him?) back in 2006 when he was the newly elected Leader of the Opposition and had just come back from paternity leave. In the intervening twelve years we've welcomed every prime minister and opposition leader bar one (Theresa May hasn't been keen so far, which is a shame; she'd find a few fellow-minded bloody difficult women), plus umpteen cabinet and shadow ministers and a broader roster running from Hillary Clinton to Meryl Streep to Russell Brand. In the glorious tradition of Diana Gould – the woman who skewered Margaret Thatcher over the sinking of the Belgrano on *Nationwide* – Mumsnet users have consistently been, to quote the *New Statesman*'s Stephen Bush, 'some of the most savage questioners any politician will face'.

It's been fascinating to watch how the guests handle it. Gordon Brown famously ignored the traditional 'what's your favourite biscuit?' question; in fact he didn't really see it because he was in old-style broadcast, not engagement mode. Hence why Mumsnetters repeated the question twelve times Jeremy Paxman-style – leading to Biscuitgate (and a mention in PMQs). In retrospect, it was one of the moments that marked the end of Westminster's control of the 'narrative'; the voters have their own microphones now, and they are not about to put them down. Those who have truly understood the switch from broadcast mode to engagement (Michael Gove, John McDonnell, Mhairi Black), and who recognise the value of unfiltered comments and questions from a highly engaged demographic, are easy to spot.

Politicians who are feeling a bit bruised can be forgiven for missing it, but humour – sly wisecracks and whimsical flights of fancy, uproarious anecdotes and flat-out filth – is our users' special sauce. From a putative toddler's internal monologue ('Earlier today I demanded that my mother get me a pear. She is by nature a difficult woman and she insisted on finishing her wee and washing her hands first') to domestic commentary ('Next-door's cat is bullying my husband'), humour is the golden thread connecting many Mumsnet users to their sanity. In combination with the anonymity of our username system, it produces no end of musings on sex and bodily functions: where else would you find hundreds of posts discussing 'fanny condensation' (any woman who's ever discussed their child's maths results while sitting on a tiny plastic chair will know exactly what this is), or – on the 'Penis beaker' thread that went so viral it broke our servers – a recommendation to 'scrub it with a wire brush and Dettol'?

It's fashionable to blame internet anonymity for all manner of ills, and of course it's almost certainly true that some people take the opportunity to say unpleasant things they'd never say face-to-face. But there's one other utterly central dimension to Mumsnet that could not exist in the same way if people could not post incognito, and that's the unstinting support and advice dispensed to those in hugely difficult or upsetting situations. Every day we see discussions that would be impossible under real-life identities, from teenage girls wanting advice on pregnancy choices, and women in violent or abusive relationships, to those facing terminal diagnoses and wondering how to tell their children. The emotional support our users provide to each other is beyond price, and the woman-centred focus is unique. For all the occasional darkness and cruelty associated with web-first networks, they are probably the truest expression there is of the diversity, pressures and complexity of real people's lives. And what really stands out is how kind people can be when the going gets rough.

The intolerable intolerance of the intolerant

Dylan Jones

For quite some time now my daughters have been telling me, 'You really can't say that.' We'll be eating at home, quite convivially, when I will inadvertently put my size 9 ½ patent leather shoe right in it. 'You can't,' my daughters will hiss at me, as one, 'define someone by their…' (deep breath) age, size, colour, nationality, sex, good looks (or not) or their (in)ability to drive, cook, write, rap, or indeed anything. At all. Both daughters are adults now, and yet they've been saying this to me for at least the last five years, maybe more in fact, and while there is often a hint of maternal irony about their condemnations (trying to protect me, in an attempt to stop me from offending anyone when I leave the sanctuary of the family home), their beliefs are real. I must not define anyone in any way that could be considered pejorative. And neither must you, or indeed anyone, come to that.

Because this is not on, at all.

Now this I get, of course, and the rather immediate and not-so-nuanced way we have now been encouraged to change our behaviour which brings with it both great emancipations and obvious challenges; most of which, however, will turn out to be beneficial to all of us, after a while at least. I remember reading an interview with the actor Tim Robbins in an American newspaper a few years ago, not long after the Harvey Weinstein story broke and as Robbins had had a number of dealings with the by-then already disgraced film producer, the interview traversed the relatively new terrain of #MeToo and #TimesUp. I don't know who brought it up, but either Robbins or the journalist mentioned a quote by Martin Amis, one I'd not heard before. Amis was discussing political correctness, and what the phrase actually meant, and the gist of which was this: we are more tolerant than our parents, and our children will turn out to be more tolerant than us – meaning that eventually we become so tolerant that we stop treating the otherness of others as a cause for concern. Or words to that effect.

However, as we all now know, one of the unfortunate by-products of this new default tolerance is an increasingly shrill intolerance towards any kind of intolerance at all. Because we are now at a point in the history of argument where any offence nullifies an argument altogether.

In the run-up to the 2018 Comment Awards (a highly influential British industry gong-fest initiated by the editor of this collection, Julia Hobsbawm), there erupted an almighty fuss which seemed determined to set back the core values of free speech by half a century. The fuss centred around identity politics and the supposed 'right not to be offended'. A month before the ceremony, two *Guardian* journalists, Gary Younge and Nesrine Malik, announced that they were withdrawing their names from the shortlist for the Society & Diversity category award because they objected to the inclusion of *The Times*'s Melanie Phillips as one of their fellow nominees. The reason, they said, was because they 'would like to draw a clear distinction between those viewpoints with which we disagree and those which we fundamentally object to on account of their bigotry and divisiveness. We believe that Phillips' body of work falls among the latter.'

This wasn't the end of it, though, as the following day, Helen Belcher, a trans activist, announced that she was asking to be removed from the Comment Awards' judging panel over the nomination of Janice Turner – another *Times* columnist – in the Commentator of the Year category. In doing so she suggested that there was a link between Turner's writings on transgenderism and 'trans suicides'. Shortly afterwards, in a rather immature act of corporate petulance, *The Times* withdrew from the whole event, telling their twelve nominated columnists not to attend.

When this final salvo landed, I commissioned one of our regular columnists, Matthew d'Ancona, to write something about it for our website. Unusually I didn't bother having a conversation about it beforehand, as I knew that not only would Matthew choose the right side of this dodecahedron (seriously, was there another option?) but also that as he is one of the most nuanced writers of his generation, that I would be able to defend his piece to the hilt. (Even though one of the principal components of a columnist's DNA is their ability and willingness to spout opinions that might have escaped [or shaken] everyone else).

As a salvo for the protection of self-expression, Matthew's column was a masterpiece. 'As the generation that was formed by the Cold War and Salman Rushdie's fatwa has been pushed aside by a new cohort of "woke" writers and intellectuals, so the primacy of free expression has been called into serious question,' he wrote. 'Safe spaces, trigger warnings and "no-platforming" have supplanted the assumption that, within the constraints of the law, free speech is paramount.'

What the fuss over the Comment Awards underscored was the fact that these days, if you offend anyone with your opinion, then by dint of that alone, your opinion has to be wrong, invalid, or at the very least, harmful to someone's feelings. As d'Ancona said himself, 'If all ideas are potentially offensive to someone – and they are – then commentary becomes almost impossible.'

This is the world we live in right now, a very small tip of a Brobdingnagian wedge, and something I wouldn't have expected from my daughters when they were still in their highchairs.

Frankly.

Freedom of speech vs licence to offend

Yasmin Alibhai-Brown

Culture wars are flaring up across the globe. The #MeToo movement has lifted the lid on seedy, repulsive male behaviours. The Weinstein allegations were first publicly made in October 2017 and a counter-offensive soon followed, led by males – particularly white males – who feel hard done by, misunderstood and victimised. Transgender people vociferously and vocally campaign for the right to self-define. Some feminists find these demands unconscionable. British Muslims are calling out for a new definition to describe the discrimination they face and British Jews are caught up in furious debates about definitions of anti-Semitism and Zionism. Racism against people of colour is evidently getting worse, but to call it out is now seen as anti-white prejudice. Migrants are scourged daily for annoying, dislocating and depriving the native sons and daughters of these isles. Those who argue for immigration are seen as elitist or unpatriotic. In this inclement climate, hostilities break out daily between opposing troops. One side weaponises freedom of speech; the other side baulks and fights back against what it sees as cruel and deplorable slurs and provocations.

No country in the world truly guarantees its citizens absolute freedom of speech or expression. No country would survive the resulting fragmentation and conflagrations. The US Constitution is seen as the torchbearer, the supreme upholder of this fundamental human right. But even in this republic of liberty, there is no settled consensus on the First Amendment. In 1952, Justice Jackson, who had been a chief prosecutor in the Nuremberg Trials, made this dissenting statement during a Supreme Court hearing about a vilely racist pamphlet, group libel and the author's right to disseminate his views: 'Abuses of freedom of expression... tear apart a society, brutalize its dominant elements and persecute, even to extermination, its minorities'. These words speak to our fractious times. But do free speech fanatics ever consider these moral arguments?

Then there are the double standards. Not one committed liberal has ever said that extremist Muslim preachers should be allowed to spout off on campuses or the media. They do not shout out for anti-Semites and paedophiles to be given a platform, either. Freedom for some and not all, it seems. This silence tells me free expression warriors do understand limits but still proclaim there cannot be limits – beyond those covered by the law.

I am with the army of resistance. In a healthy democracy, citizens and public figures should feel able to express strong views which challenge received wisdom or defy groupthink. A good society is a free society. But there are limits: legal, professionally determined, authorised and unspoken. And yet fundamentalist liberals still pretend that these restrictions don't exist, that 'British values' entitle us all to say what we damn well like, even if that debilitates individuals or ignites discord. This barbaric twenty-first-century blood sport is neither entertaining nor harmless. As I write in my new book, *In Defence of Political Correctness*: hateful commentaries and comments in the public spaces are ripping us apart. We should, apparently, just shut up and put up with foul words and unfair assertions. Object to these and you are disdainfully dismissed as 'PC' or abject, one of those who is too easily affronted. Just because everyone seems to be taking offence doesn't mean that no one should ever be offended. Sure, sometimes too much noise and emotions explode over minor utterances. Such overreaction is counterproductive. Those of us who believe in civility and restraint need to be mindful of that. However, those who will not temper what they say and how they say it do far more damage.

I wonder if the shocking number of people now suffering from mental illness and distress is linked to the unrestrained discourse all around us and online. Arguably, speech can cut more deeply into a person's sense of self than brute violence. As Shakespeare's Coriolanus says: 'When blows have made me stay, I fled from words'.

We see all around us the results of free speech zealotry. Trump's victory, Brexit, Erdogan's rise to power, Modi's Hinduized India, the Wahabi takeover of Islam, nativism and populism are destabilising the centres of stable democracies. Some call this 'necessary disruption', a means by which we will get a more democratic and open idyll. This is delusional and dangerous. Thank heaven for those young women and men, particularly in our universities, who have valiantly been resisting and defying these new norms. Wake up, liberals. While you go on your free speech jihads, females, gay people and various minorities feel the burn. The columnist Fintan O'Toole believes we are living in pre-Fascist times. He is right. Remember the words of Judge Jackson. Speech, some seemingly mild, normalised the hatred of 'The Other' in the Weimar Republic, in Bosnia, in Rwanda. You know what came next.

Policy can change the inequalities gap

Adrian Monck

'When Davos gets the story but the BBC ignores it', left-wing firebrand Paul Mason tweeted recently, sharing a World Economic Forum story on inequality. The story featured the work of Professor Philip Alston, United Nations Special Rapporteur on extreme poverty and human rights. Everyone knew what Mason meant. Even the people behind Davos get inequality. Even the elites get it.

Even I get it. (Small disclosure, I work for the World Economic Forum.) Researchers at London's Imperial College just announced that the life expectancy of England's poorest women has fallen since 2011. To quote Professor Alston: 'the full picture of low-income wellbeing in the UK cannot be captured by statistics alone.' So perhaps I can share my story.

It is four years this December since one of those 'poorest women' died. She was my sister. My phone was on as my plane taxied to its stand in Paris. The call was as brief as it was unexpected. Next year, I had told myself, was *the* year, after so many years, that we would finally be in touch again. It never happened. She was found in the bedroom of a seaside guest house that entrepreneurship had transformed into a care home. Forty-six years old. I sat in an arrivals corridor at Charles de Gaulle, on one of those cold plastic seats no one ever uses, and wept as people hurried past.

Undertakers and autopsies go slowly over Christmas, so it wasn't until January – Davos time for me – that she got her slot at Great Yarmouth's crematorium. Blue velvet curtains opened and shut, the cinema-style organ played, and then the flowers were bundled up to make way for the next set of chrysanthemum wreaths. Sandwiches on the seafront. That was my sister's life done.

Here is how inequality works. I was her older brother. I made it to the good school, the one that didn't throw you out at sixteen. She struggled with learning difficulties and bullying. I made it to university, she made it to the benefits system. I got married, she ended up a victim of domestic violence. I put myself through an MBA, she was sectioned. I ate out all the time but got thinner. She didn't.

She would always struggle. Education. Income. And the biggest struggle? Health. She was diagnosed with paranoid schizophrenia. She had diabetes. Her lack of education left her unworldly, an easy prey to slick advertising, point of sale product placement, and unable to make what health professionals call 'the right choices'.

In *Scientific American* recently, Stanford neuroscientist Robert Sapolsky wrote about the 'health-wealth gap'. In *The Lancet* medical experts call it 'psychosocial stress': the way in which poverty devours the poor alive. But grateful as I am for them, I don't need academic studies to tell me that inequality poisons every outcome in a person's life: schooling, opportunities, relationships, health.

And I don't need Paul Mason to remind me that even I get it.

Can organisations like mine help? One of the books that will surely be on the Christmas recommendation list is *Winners Take All: The Elite Charade of Changing the World*. The author, Anand Giridharadas, launches an excoriating attack on talking shops, conferences, think tanks and policy shops. He has a point.

But tackling inequality requires not just our outrage at lives cut short and opportunities lost. It also requires the slow, constant drip of attention. It requires inequality to be put in front of business and political leaders year after year after year. It requires the well-meaning conveners of panels, the kindly collectors of data on topics like inclusive growth, that can be turned into policy recommendations for politicians. Policy will not bring my sister back, but policy can close the fatal gap.

My unspun heroes

Anthony Seldon

Journalists need to understand what is happening behind closed doors at the heart of politics and government if they are going to tell their readers anything new. This uncovering is crucial at all times, but never more so than now, with Britain in the midst of the biggest political melee; teetering on the verge of the biggest constitutional crisis since the arrival of popular democracy exactly a hundred years ago.

How can journalists find out what is really happening behind those closed doors? If they just want to give us the benefit of their opinions, then inside knowledge of what is going on is hardly important. They can even make it up, as some working for papers, internet outlets and broadcasters *do*, knowing that those in the know don't want to get sucked into denial.

Few manage to penetrate deep into the heart of 24-hour politics and government to give us genuinely fresh knowledge. In the absence of leaked or intercepted documents, these journalists must rely on oral evidence. It can be given at open briefings or confidentially, in face-to-face meetings in discreet locations, down secure phone lines or through private social media. Finding out what is really going on is not easy.

Decisions have become increasingly focused in the last 30 years within Number 10. The Home Office, Foreign Office and Ministry of Defence are vassal states of Downing Street. The Treasury retains some independence, notably when the Chancellor has independent standing, as did Gordon Brown (1997–2007) and George Osborne (2010–16).

But if journalists do not know what the prime minister and their close team are thinking and doing, their articles and reports will be very thin. The 1980s was the decade when Margaret Thatcher's right-hand official on foreign policy, Charles Powell, and equally close press secretary, Bernard Ingham, tightened the grip of the centre across Whitehall.

Number 10 does not like its secrets to be known. It punishes political aides who leak, and they know it. Why jeopardise the best job many will ever have by chatting to journalists as they used to do when they were in Whitehall departments or working for lesser politicians on their way up? Civil servants prone to leaking would never make it into the building in the first place. The system would have quietly weeded them out.

To get on in Number 10 dictates loyalty to the political boss and chiefs. That means that whatever the journalists are told, either in lobby briefings or bilaterally, will be told for a particular reason. It is the job of the Number 10 employees to protect the prime minister and to put their policy across in the most favourable light.

That means that when it has stories to give out, a new policy initiative, perhaps, or news of a visit to the White House, they go to those who are loyal at worst, or who play a straight bat at best. Alastair Campbell, who headed Number 10's communications for Tony Blair from 1997 to 2003, was a master at using information as a secret weapon, feeding some journalists while punishing others.

Obtaining trust from Number 10 is never easy. And it is a mixed blessing. It can be gained with the administration of one political party, only for the journalists to find themselves out in the cold when another party takes over. It can be worse when a new prime minister from the same party takes over. Journalists who were in with the Blair court suddenly found themselves flung out in the cold when Gordon Brown took over in June 2007.

Not many journalists are able to keep close to Number 10 through transitions. James Margach at *The Sunday Times* was close to Number 10 through three changes of prime minister during the 13 years of Conservative governments from 1951 to 1964. David Watt of the *Financial Times* managed to penetrate deep inside Downing Street through transitions, as did Hugo Young of the *Sunday Times* and the *Guardian*, and Peter Jenkins who wrote also for both titles as well as for the *Independent*.

Looking back through the press cuttings, it can be relatively easy to see which journalists got it, and who allowed themselves to be spun as useful idiots by insiders. In less scrupulous outlets across all media forms, editors often put sales-worthy sensation or purity to the party line of the organ above objective truth. The EU divide, which goes back in earnest to the Maastricht debates in the early 1990s, has seen standards of objective reporting fall particularly low.

Over that whole 25-year period, which corresponds with the time I have been writing my five books on PMs, based on over 1,500 recorded interviews, getting politicians and aides to stop talking and spinning has at times been a problem, but it is the officials who lay the golden eggs. When reading back over cuttings, I have unsurprisingly found the middle-ground press the most consistently insightful – *The Times*, *The Sunday Times* and the *Financial Times*. That said, it is a journalist from the *Observer*, Andrew Rawnsley, who has been the single most illuminating, along with Tim Shipman of *The Sunday Times* most recently. Like the best, they write books, as have all the journalists mentioned by name above. They write English so well, too.

Why a real diversity of opinion is essential to the survival of comment

Claire Fox

Diversity is all the rage. Unless it is diversity of opinion. That is a problem for those who commission a diverse range of opinion pieces. Try as they might to ensure comment pages are not just echo chambers that trot out beautifully written but same-y columns, we live in a culture of conformity that lashes out when faced with heterodox views. The havoc wreaked on the Comment Awards by today's identity warriors at the end of 2018 is just one example. This is a growing trend.

Even challenging identity politics is a contentious comment-too-far for some. In the wake of Donald Trump's election, the *New York Times* published an article by Mark Lilla, a professor of humanities at Columbia University. In a stinging rebuke to his own liberal tribe for facilitating the new president's accession to the White House entitled 'The End of Identity Liberalism', Lilla explained why so many in the media were blindsided by the election result: 'The fixation on diversity in our schools and in the press has produced a generation of liberals and progressives narcissistically unaware of conditions outside their self-defined groups, and indifferent to the task of reaching out to Americans in every walk of life.' The opinion piece went viral, but also led to a backlash. Lilla was savaged by critics such as his own colleague Katherine Franke, who argued that 'Lilla's op-ed does the... nefarious background work of making white supremacy respectable', accusing him of 'contributing to the same ideological project' as former Klan leader David Duke and the KKK. So, writing a column tackling identity politics can get you labelled as an enabler of white supremacism.

Perhaps taking Lilla's hint, the *NYT* subsequently hired a number of comment writers from beyond the liberal, progressive comfort zone. This has not gone down well. In 2017, the paper hired former *Wall Street Journal* and Pulitzer Prize-winning columnist Bret Stephens as part of 'a public commitment to reflecting a broader range of perspectives in its pages... of busting up the mostly liberal echo chamber'. There was a furious response and a campaign to cancel subscriptions. Stephens, a conservative (although scathing critic of Trump), is a critic of what he describes as the 'near-religious fervor with which the climate-advocacy community seeks to win converts and castigate heretics as morally abominable people'. As such he was denounced as an 'extreme climate science denier'. Many called for him to be fired. One critic demanded that if 'the *New York Times* values truth... care(s) about their credibility... they will sack him'. Sack him, said so casually, is becoming a worryingly prevalent reaction to writers whose copy doesn't fit into a narrow straightjacket of received opinion.

There was similar hostility when another former *Wall Street Journal* writer, Bari Weiss, joined the *NYT* opinion section. Her dissenting views on the excesses of the new PC orthodoxy, for example on #MeToo and cultural appropriation, has triggered regular denunciations. One of Weiss's detractors had a pop at the *NYT* by arguing, 'People at the paper like to talk about the hires as matters of intellectual rigor and viewpoint diversity, but all they're doing is draping a philosopher's toga around a troll'. So, diverse views that don't conform are written off as trolling.

Now real trolls are leading risk-adverse publishers to introduce chilling 'morality clauses'. It was recently revealed that

Condé Nast magazines' yearly contracts for regular contributors state that, if in the company's 'sole judgment', a writer 'becomes the subject of public disrepute, contempt, complaints or scandals', Condé Nast can terminate the agreement: 'In other words, a writer need not have done anything wrong... In the age of the Twitter mob, that could mean simply writing or saying something that offends some group of strident tweeters'.

Beyond such contractual threats, a sinister new corporate bullying hangs over comment writers, to keep their copy inoffensive. In February 2018 Richard Littlejohn wrote a column in the *Daily Mail* in reaction to Tom Daley and Dustin Lance Black's 'flaunting the ultrasound scans of their unborn child' under the provocative headline: 'Please don't pretend two dads is the new normal'. There was much in the article to disagree with, but campaigners didn't argue back or even confine themselves to shouting homophobia. Instead Stop Funding Hate mass-tweeted at businesses, leading to the likes of Center Parcs, Paperchase and Pizza Hut being pressurised to stop advertising in the *Mail*. If comment is to survive, especially when the printed press needs advertisers, we need to oppose 'progressives' using big-business stage armies to dictate what articles are written.

Worryingly, such censorious trends are becoming fashionable amongst journalists themselves, who increasingly police what topics are open for comment. Take the case of American essayist Katie Roiphe. Her comment piece on #MeToo, written for *Harper's* magazine, became the subject of a huge outrage-fest in January 2018, two months *before* it was due to be published. It was writers and editors at *Harper's* who began a Twitter campaign, warning (mistakenly as it turned out) that the article would reveal the identity of the person who'd anonymously compiled the 'Shitty Media Men' list – a spreadsheet that named and shamed allegedly predatory men in the media. One might hope journalists would aim their fire at a blacklist of unproven rumours against their peers. Instead they furiously targeted

Roiphe for being critical of such a list. Writers publicly pulled stories from *Harper's* to pressure the magazine not to publish the piece. Despite not having read it, the *Guardian*'s Jessica Valenti described Roiphe's article as 'incredibly dangerous' and tweeted *Harper's* phone number to allow people to hassle the publishers.

Roiphe's article was eventually published. But reviling, often slandering fellow journalists can exact a terrible price. Disgracefully, distinguished *New York Review of Books* editor Ian Buruma was forced to resign after commissioning a 'verboten' article (again related to #MeToo) after a savage pile-on led by media professionals. How can we explain this shameful, censorious betrayal of a free press from within journalistic ranks? Writing of the Buruma case, Colin Marshall explains that new generations of journalists are swayed by 'ideological fads and political fashions' as they've 'grown up... with the conception of an educated person as someone possessed, not of a particular body of knowledge, but an approved suite of opinions'. Such an intolerant journalistic culture, that only approves of comment that narrowly fits into a prescriptive 'approved suite of opinions', could mean comment writers signing their own death warrants. And for readers, who wants sanitised, anodyne, clichéd copy that ticks the right boxes but is homogeneous and safe? Here's to REAL diversity if comment is to survive.

Can we heal our divided country?

Deborah Mattinson

Towards the end of 2018 I asked focus groups to choose just three words to describe contemporary Britain. The question produced an assortment of negatives: 'disappointing', 'struggling', 'fearful', 'claustrophobic', 'distorted' and 'unequal' give the flavour, but the word that came up most frequently was 'divided' – and eight out of ten of us believe that Britain will become still more divided in the year ahead.

We are divided by age, gender, geography, class and education. This is partly about economic inequality: 64 per cent of us describe ourselves as 'have-nots'. Focus group participants in small towns all around the UK spontaneously describe their area as a 'left behind community', adopting the vocabulary of policy makers with terrifying ease. These deep divisions are also rooted in cultural and values differences. We are as divided by our views on feminism, religion, climate change, the death penalty or gay rights as we are by where we live or went to college.

Many commentators talk as if Brexit itself brought about these divisions. Certainly, the result of the 2016 vote shone a light on just how differently certain groups see the world and Britain's role within it, but those differences and the attitudes that lay behind them speak to a much longer-term trend. As the referendum campaign wore on, the sense of fragmentation became more powerful, while, at the same time, each side found it harder and harder to comprehend the others' perspectives. In particular, 'Remainers', typically the commentariat and Westminster bubble, assumed that their view was the dominant world view. As those Remainers licked their wounds after the result one Leave voter in a focus group told me how much he had enjoyed 'sticking two fingers up to the elites'.

Curiously, the Brexit negotiation process had the effect of uniting disparate groups on some issues. Immediately after the referendum BritainThinks established its 'Brexit Diaries' project where 100 voters in 10 UK locations (52 Leavers and 48 Remainers) kept diaries recording their spontaneous thoughts as events unfolded. Initially, while Remainers were predictably gloomy, Leavers were joyful and positive, optimistic about the best possible outcome for the UK. However, as the months passed by, increasingly all agreed that the talks were going badly. It became harder to distinguish Leavers' and Remainers' comments as everyone became similarly downcast.

There was consensus, too, about the political response, with most feeling that neither of the two main party leaders were up to the job. There was a sense that the problems that the country faced were growing larger and affecting more and more people: high cost of living, housing shortages, rising crime, precarious employment and most of all, failing public services. I began to hear anecdotal evidence about the impact of cuts in schools (large class sizes, poorly trained teachers, lack of exercise books and textbooks) and hospitals (dirty wards, long waiting lists, cancelled operations) that I had not heard since the mid 1990s. The difference is that back then people believed that politicians were focused on the problems, and they were at the centre of national conversation. Now it seems that Brexit has overshadowed everything and sucked energy away from debate on anything else.

It is not just that Brexit seems less tangible, and pertinent to voters' lives than issues like health, education and crime: quite frankly, most voters are bored with Brexit. Even Leave voters, who voted a year and a half ago with a spring in their step, looking for a new way of doing politics, now see Brexit as symbolic of the worst of politics as usual, rather than the refreshing change that they had hoped for. Against this backdrop, it seems unlikely that Brexit will do much to address the long-term erosion of trust in 'elites'.

By the time this essay is published some of the Brexit unknowns will be known. It is hard to predict how this will end up, but what I can predict, given the diversity of public attitudes, is that the outcome is unlikely to please – or even satisfy – everyone. Asked to look ahead to 2019, voters, at the end of 2018, said that, more than anything, they wanted the country to 'come together'. It is hard to see how that can happen, wherever the Brexit negotiations and subsequent votes take us – until the deep-rooted inequalities and value differences that led to Brexit in the first place have been addressed.

It's the climate, stupid

Ed Gillespie

A decade is a long time in the context of climate change. In dark irony it's also practically all we have left to make the necessary transition. The days of climate deniers shrieking 'warmists!' at scientists, accusing every activist of ideological leanings of being 'watermelons' (green on the outside, red on the inside) and claiming that for climate change campaigners such as George Monbiot and Nasa's Jim Hansen, 'hanging is too good for such ineffable toe rags', are hopefully behind us.

The climate sceptics have been understandably quiet in recent months, as wildfires killed hundreds in raging infernos first in Portugal, then Greece, then California. Even the boreal forests of Scandinavia dried dangerously into tinderbox conditions in the oppressive summer heat. FUD (fear, uncertainty and doubt) tactics tend to flounder when the palpable flames of evidence are licking at the threshold. The real fear is here and that fear is real. Even the *Sun* declared 'the world is on fire!'. A climate denier has yet to start an insurance company in defiance of these losses. We await the day.

It's hard to admit how wrong we have been and for how long. Concerns about burning billions of years of fossilised sunshine in the blink of a geological eye are almost as old as the industrial revolution that first raised them. Climate change is not a black swan, something that takes us by surprise, with massive far-reaching impacts like 9/11, it is a white swan that has been swimming towards us with grim, relentless predictability for over a century. Where has the effective commentary been on that?

The progress achieved through the harnessing of relatively cheap, available and abundant fossil fuels has been extraordinary. But when the pursuit of further progress by the same means is creating the climatic changes that threaten all future progress, a so-called 'progress trap', then doing things differently is not just preferential, it's existential. This is the grist. That our very system might be suicidal is difficult to absorb. It is the sharpest cognitive dissonance for our core beliefs. As Lemn Sissay says in his poem 'What if?':

Let me get it right. What if we got it wrong?

What if we weakened ourselves getting strong?

Little wonder then that the 'shock' of this revelation has built to a shrill crescendo over umpteen Intergovernmental Panel on Climate Change (IPCC) reports and increasingly desperate and fevered Conference of the Parties (COP) summits, like the most recent in the dark winter days of late 2018 in Katowice, Poland. Sponsored by a coal company. History may laugh sardonically at our lack of a civilisational sense of irony. Contrarian commentary loves to fly, probably on Ryanair, in the face of this consolidated opinion.

Because this is beyond ideology now. The science is as 'done' as science ever can be. Those who screech 'paradigm' and claim orthodoxy is strangling reality are not just outliers; they are like alchemists claiming that because no one has turned base metal to gold, doesn't mean it can't be done. It might in principle be possible that the Anthropocene is not destabilising our climate to an existential extent, but in manifest practice it is looking extremely unlikely.

In a system as complex as global climate there will always be anomalies and inconsistencies, just as there are always exceptional, 'miraculous' cancer survivors. But as Sir Paul Nurse put it to James Delingpole in what I think is still a seminal moment in climate commentary: 'If a dear relative was suffering from a fatal disease, would you opt for the "consensus" treatment recommended by doctors or advise to drink more orange juice offered by a fringe maverick quack?' To which Delingpole screamed 'intellectual rape' and formally complained to the BBC. The consensus is pretty much unequivocally in. Now let's comment and debate on our response to the diagnosis. Those prescribing 'more of the same' are like the doctors backing fag adverts.

'In whose interests?' is the burning question. When supposed 'think tanks' refuse to divulge their funding sources we are in deep trouble. The climate action we need will involve winners and losers. That much is inevitable. But we cannot let the losers, like the fossil fuel businesses, dictate the pace of change. That way lies the fast track to Armageddon. With 'sustainable' shareholder returns.

Public support for climate action is consistently strong, albeit with the usual caveats of concerns over the economy, health service and education. But perhaps if the truly systemic nature of the jolt needed was comprehended, we'd realise that we could reboot almost everything, from energy generation, through transport to food production and build a resilient economy that also served people and the environment. That is actually simpler than rocket science.

Twelve years is how long the IPCC says we have to make the shift required. But it is not a dozen years *until* we change. That's how long we have to *make* the change. Every month matters. A decade or two of obfuscation and stalling has only intensified our task and made it much harder. We're entering a massive chicane. A pinch-point. The window of opportunity is small and the time is short. The countdown drum beat has begun.

As Churchill said: 'Owing to past neglect, in the face of the plainest warnings, we have now entered upon a period of danger... The era of procrastination, of half-measures, of soothing and baffling expedients, of delays, is coming to its close. In its place we are entering a period of consequences.' The moment for 'peace in our time' has passed. Which is why the emergence of movements like the Extinction Rebellion are timely; 'Tell the truth. And act like that truth is real,' is a reasonable demand in unreasonable times. The essential transition happens on our watch. In our careers. In our lives. It needs to be radical.

This transformation could be transcendent. Raising a traditionally narrow-minded nationalism of 'blood and soil' to one blood, one earth. Climate change is a test of our civilisational maturity. It's likely any intelligent, curious species such as ours will eventually bump up against the limits of its planetary environment. It is how we respond that is critical. Caught in the perpetual melee of the fierce urgency of now, me, here, over the timeless, global 'we'. Maybe this is our curse?

Knowingly allowing the true hideousness of climate change to unfold is technically genocide, and the biggest in history. Any commentary that obfuscates this is complicit. Let the debate on solutions commence. But let's deflate the Ozymandian arrogance that got us here. And also appreciate that climate chaos is driving desperate migration that will turn from a trickle to a flood unless we act decisively and in ways that are often politically uncomfortable. The alternative is nightmarish.

King Cnut was infamously misinterpreted. Sitting enthroned below the high tide line, his alleged arrogance was inundated by the rising waters. In fact he originally set out to humbly demonstrate the inability of humanity to resist the inevitable elements. Only now he is wrong. We can and are influencing those elements consciously, and to the detriment of all. We are the first generation in history to be simultaneously aware of our potentially fatal civilisational dilemma, whilst having the means to resolve it. It's a live and real choice. We fix this together or all go down together. Those who continue to claim otherwise are a bunch of Cnuts.

Comment is the skeleton key to understanding

Geraldine Sharpe-Newton

Editorial Intelligence's launch of the Comment Awards a decade ago has led to a revealing scrutiny of comment journalism. I believe the once narrow and specific attention to Comment journalism has blossomed and changed. In our future we must also embrace some remarkable and recent developments.

It's clear from one glance at the epic list of those who trade in the basic art of comment and those who have joined them with its variants, that it is the variants which have nourished and stimulated the art. Certainly, most newspapers and magazines should be applauded for having subtly found a new route towards the development of comment journalism.

I believe we are now seeing a development beyond pure journalism that is desperately needed if our beloved magazines and newspapers are to survive and grow. After all, readers don't just read, or thumb through a daily, weekly or monthly simply to know what's happening now. They read to understand. But they also read because 'they want to know what to think and why'. Even perhaps, how to talk about what they have read.

In this sense, I believe comment is more than ever the gold standard of much of our journalism. Some newspapers are still passing through a stage of crude, slightly shouty simplicity, encouraging viewers, listeners and readers to 'have a go', to make their own not very well-thought-out comments. There is no shortage of that. Dig around in some popular tabloids and you will discover the delectable 'angry buttons' that ordinary mortals love to press and repeat. The embrace of this rhetoric is seldom constructive or instructive. Some grand newspapers appear to enjoy what they call a 'modern story of dirty money and ultra-wealthy miscreants'. In fact, their delectable 'Hot Button' is often money, egotism and greed, especially when attached to a slightly raunchy 'high street villain'.

These kinds of comment are simple, understandable, attractive and easy to repeat on the bus, or when waiting for the Deliveroo pizza bike to arrive. But they do not bring readers to what Editorial Intelligence would embrace as 'a proper level of understanding'. It's clear that readers are discovering how much more subtle and complex everything is, and how much more subtle and clever the journalism has had to become, to reflect it. Because we are experiencing a process of gradual, confusing and perhaps unconscious assimilation of facts, ideas and knowledge, one tends to think, 'so much to read' and that makes every issue and problem harder to handle.

For years now, *The Economist* has managed to condense and clarify to a high degree and has taken comment along on the journey. Somehow those clever, unnamed people dotted round the world routinely bring clarity to bear on the confusion. In 2017, when I gave the Chairman's Award to *The Economist*, it was because they had routinely achieved the seemingly impossible. Splicing together the frighteningly disruptive, contradictory, confidence-crushing machinations of a confused world.

Refreshingly and increasingly, comment is not just about thought, experienced analysis and well-strung words on a narrow range of subjects. We must accept that cartoons, sport, film review and more are all part of the comment stable.

Well-written reviews of the film *First Man* have made it above the 'comment horizon' to explain that the straight-faced portrayal of Neil Armstrong was much less a tale of simple adventure, but more acutely a portrait of solid, dogged, calculated and straight-faced leadership.

At another level and across all newspapers and magazines you will find cleverly crafted cartoons that also take 'comment' to a new level, beyond the jokes. The weekly *New Yorker* magazine in particular has increasingly elevated the cartoon to the level of edgy social and political comment. Recently in the *Times Literary Supplement*, above a review of Andrew Roberts' epic biography of Winston Churchill, was a beautiful Lowe cartoon from 1954. It shows a dozen or so different, all insistently powerful and mockingly in charge, versions of Churchill. It provided more than any comment, or even Roberts' 1,000-page opus, could possibly hope to embrace.

In the sports pages, you find elegant writers, increasingly worthy of our attention, bringing subtle insights to bear as comment. Recently in the *Telegraph*, a comment piece elegantly introduced us to the strange world of goalkeepers. It ranked, compared, rated and explained them, way beyond simple reportage. The collapse of the José Mourinho era at Manchester United has recently elevated simple reporting to new levels of elegant comment.

What is happening is that the comment sections of papers and magazines are thriving, but without necessarily being directly under the banner of comment. Writers from across the landscape are aspiring to new levels of excellence and are taking journalism, good old-fashioned, fact-based 'hackery', along with them.

It's lazy to suggest that the better the facts, the better the understanding, the better the comment. There is a danger here. The wealth of thought and information being presented to us, tailored, ideally to suit different age groups, beliefs and temperaments, are simply creating new and daunting 'silos' of thought. Apologies for introducing reference to the 'silo mentality', but it is unavoidable. So often in old-fashioned 'man-bites-dog' journalism, one part of the story might not easily share information or facts with another part of the story, so for a variety of reasons will be ignored.

What I love is to be surprised by a fresh thought in a comment column, but I also believe readers who care could slip dangerously into an overload of choice and thus be forced back into their comfort zone. This clearly became so with many angry Brexiteers.

There is a great risk that we neglect our 'worldly thought' and understanding. So we must all be concerned with how we educate the young. Thinking through ideas, commenting on current issues, exploring stories, bringing words to life, discovering the unexpected, delighting in argument, and reveling in those 'aha' moments. I firmly believe that comment has the power to generate the thoughts and ideas that create 'connectivity', and if we are lucky maybe we can build a structure of thought. I shall leave what I call e-comment to others. The business of tweets, Facebook, of 'black-ops' and their 'nuclear' children, their inherent threats and risks to fact and information manipulation are so complicatedly separate, they must be treated elsewhere.

It's encouraging to note that comment as text, photograph, graphic, cartoon or more is so often what we reach for after we have spent diligent time with the front-page facts of hard news. Thus, we break a deadlock and bring proper relief, understanding and journalistic clarity to a story. Comment journalism is the ultimate 'skeleton key' to any level of proper understanding.

The bitter and shallow battles of the Brexit debate

Gisela Stuart

Introducing his radio series 'Living with the Gods', Neil MacGregor reflected that if you have gods, then they can disagree which each other, make mistakes and fight it out. If there is only one god, then the unexpected or imperfect can only be explained in terms of sin and sinners. Listening to him I could not help but draw parallels between his radio series and our current political discourse.

After the United Kingdom's decision to leave the European Union we seem to have turned away from considering competing ideas and have just labelled people as good or bad. The merits of the decision about the UK's democratic structures and governance were being countered by arguments based on the 'just-in-time supply chain' requirements of large multinational companies. The underlying question of whether it is liberal democracies that create the conditions for economic prosperity or that accountability and self-determination are just something 'nice to have' once you have made enough money was never aired. Unless we give up the right to make our own laws, 'we will be poorer' continues to be the strapline.

This merry-go-round of 'good people' shouting at 'bad people', telling them that they are ignorant, racist and/or gullible has been going on since the summer of 2016. Those who lost demand from those who won that they better explain themselves. There is little evidence of opinion shifting on the ground. The general election in 2017 reduced the government's majority, but the party that pledged to overturn the referendum was one of the biggest losers on the day.

The good people have failed to convert the bad people and the bad people still don't see anything wrong with having voted to leave the European Union. Some have become noisier whilst others have withdrawn into the silence of their private thoughts. Perversely it is the progressives who are harking back to the sunny uplands before Brexit. Some novel ideas are emerging. As the winning side had greater support from older voters, the young could just wait for them to die, and in time claim demographic victory.

How did the world's sixth largest economy with a reputation for political stability and administrative competence get itself into this mess?

People join or vote for political parties that broadly reflect their views. General elections measure the relative support for competing ideas, and after the ballot those elected get together, and whilst holding the winning party to account, broadly aim to allow the government to function. Parliamentary sovereignty is understood to be about curtailing a powerful executive, not treating the voters as if they were a political opponent.

Unexpected results aren't new, but the system is used to dealing with them – the coalition government in 2010 being the most recent example. The use of referenda is a more recent development, but no one baulked at the first EU referendum in the 1970s, the Scottish referenda, the Welsh referenda or the vote on replacing First Past the Post with AV. But 2016 was just so different.

A once-in-a-generation ballot, on a voter turnout of 72 per cent with a winning margin of 3.8 per cent, exposed ever-deepening divisions, resulting in the breakdown of established structures. Every single component of our parliamentary democracy is being challenged and found wanting. It won't be resolved anytime soon, because the age of unchecked globalisation and unquestioned liberal values is being challenged everywhere.

Neither of the two main political parties have resolved their deep, and long-existing, divisions over Europe. Both parties are led by people who appear to defend positions which do not chime with what they have said in the past about the EU. The prime minister has not shown the imagination needed to harness the opportunities of our departure from the EU. The leader of the opposition, who has been a longstanding Eurosceptic, focuses on the manner of our leaving rather than the decision itself. To be fair, the government's negotiation strategy provides plenty of scope for legitimate criticism.

None of the options of leaving are said to have sufficient support and parliament is said to be poised to wrench power away from the government and take back control. The very people who for more than two years have spent their energies explaining that leaving is just too difficult and – *sotto voce* – we should never have voted to leave in the first place.

Parliament decided to ask voters a direct question and has not come to terms with the fact that it neither anticipated nor liked the answer it got. The political parties, the engines that forge consensus and enable compromises to be reached, are split along new fault lines. The fierce debates are internal, excluding the voters who feel that they have made their decision.

The debate has become heated, personal and unpleasant, but that's because there is so little intellectual substance to it. Democratic politics is facing a revolutionary upheaval. The sooner MPs, parliament and commentators inside the M25 bubble realise there is something wrong with them, not with the people, the better.

Lucky me

Jane Brien

They don't have liberal arts schools in England, they have 'uni', and if you wanted to go to uni there was only one option after failing your exams – retaking your exams. That meant a gruelling year at a 'crammer'; places run by wannabe professors who earn a living bullying the underachieving children of middle-class parents with rote memorisation of Shakespearean passages, equations, dates and treaties.

Instead, I left school and spent a year visiting my more disciplined friends at their chosen seats of higher learning. I stayed with those who had so skilfully distracted me from my own studies. At Bristol, where Sarah was studying psychology, I slept on the floor and became the stage manager of a play at the student union (I think they just assumed I was a student). I helped my friend Ailsa clean out the mouse cages in the lab at Sussex where she was reading Animal Behaviour and I brought a cache of magic mushrooms to Fiona and Soph who were reading Linguistics at Edinburgh. I didn't go to many classes, but those I did attend were huge lectures in rooms that looked like they were made for the UN Security Council.

After having spent a year as an ersatz uni student travelling around the UK, my mother suggested I might want to look at an American liberal arts school – their admission requirements can be a little more forgiving. She had a friend who taught at a liberal arts college in New York's Hudson Valley; a famous philandering philosopher who married the same woman twice and whose son was almost as academically unremarkable as me. She thought if they let Nick in they would surely have a place for her daughter.

A college reputation is like radioactive waste; it should be measured in half-lives. If a college had become known for something sixty years ago it will still be half-known for the same thing sixty years on. This particular college, in the lush Hudson River Valley, was once dubbed 'The Little Red Whorehouse' by gossip columnist Walter Winchell after his daughter apparently got pregnant on a weekend campus visit in 1958. That moniker was still in the ether when I visited.

I arrived at Bard at the end of January 1985. My dormitory was an Italianate wedding cake mansion on the south-west side of campus. It was a supposedly haunted, women-only dorm and my room had a working fireplace and a balcony. In my suitcase I had brought a leopard-skin blanket, a gold sparkling net to hang over the bed, three wigs and some ratty clothes. I had long purple hair and an orange fake fur coat made by Princess Diana's sister's nanny.

My roommate had spent January in France on a French immersion programme that seemed to involve buying lots of lingerie in Paris and hooking up with guys from other colleges. She returned after I moved in and immediately took a dislike to me. The first words she ever said to me were: 'Do you know how to get blood and semen out of silk?' I didn't.

One of my earliest classes was First Year Seminar, a cornerstone of the Bard curriculum. It was held in a tiny basement room. Not designed as a classroom, more like a utility room, the ceiling was latticed with ducts and pipes, some that had been labelled by previous japester students 'bong water expulsion system'. Everyone smoked in my class, including the professor – she had the remarkable ability to have one in her hand, one attached to her lip and one going in the ashtray all at the same time. There were no windows. It seemed not to be customary to put your hand up to ask to leave the room, so if you needed or just wanted to leave, you got up to go and came back, or not, sometime later.

That particular professor was said to be the model for Martha in Edward Albee's *Who's Afraid of Virginia Woolf*, a story which thrilled me, as unlikely as it was to be true. I took a Shakespeare class with her in my junior year, where one day her husband, also a Shakespeare scholar, came into class and they proceeded to get into a raging fight in front of us about the interpretation of Kate's transformation in *The Taming of the Shrew*. Lots of spluttering and stuttering and name calling, 'Oh for God's sake, don't be so ridiculous, that is preposterous, you are a fool, she's not a feminist – I'm a feminist'.

For the first time I was taking myself seriously and succeeding in my classes; it was a revelation. My selections were all over the map, one minute I was an Irish literature major, the next I was master electrician in the theatre, then I was taking welding until I got into a fight with the sexist ex-marine sculpture professor, then it was women's studies and history. The liberal arts lets you do all of these things and I loved it. I even started loving Americans, realising they weren't all people who had shot John Lennon and said words like 'awesome,' 'nauseous' and 'totally'.

Bard was also weird and wild, and the legacy of the crazy days of the 1970s, when the college almost went bankrupt and students studied in the 'Inner College' that was taught mostly up a tree, still lingered. My sophomore year I took a class called Forming 1; a class with no syllabus or grades, you went into a room and did something, anything. There was possibly music and sometimes not. There was a professor and sometimes not. Once there was a dance involving toilet paper, another time someone said the word 'tree' for an hour. There was also Forming 2 and 3, but I didn't take those. My criteria report sheet from the professor at mid-term said, 'We have begun, now let us begin'.

No country is perfect, but in 2018 the US seems to be leading the world in personal, political and environmental degradation, yet the model of the US liberal arts college perseveres. Liberal arts colleges might just be the best thing about America.

The comment bull and bear market

Julia Hobsbawm

Picture the scene. Two mainstream newspaper columnists urge their readers to impose strict digital diets on themselves because of the psychological harm it causes and to basically stop consuming media – or at least heavily restrict it. The sub-head on Janice Turner's *Times* column in December 2018 read 'we've been turned into iPhone crackheads' whilst over in the *Guardian* a few months before Jonathan Freedland had urged his readers to stop using social media and have a digital detox because 'the problem lies not with abuse of the medium, but with the medium itself'.

This was all a world away from a decade before when everyone loved the digital, loved our days being invigorated by the way ideas and comment could be shared at such network scale and proliferate on someone else's medium. Back then, the 'always on' era was welcome.

Back then, in 2009, the broadcast regulator Ofcom was not yet publishing data showing that the average Briton checks their phone every twelve minutes (which is eighty separate episodes during every waking hour). Back then, Twitter was a toddler, Instagram was still a twinkle in a Silicon Valley eye, and Blackberry was still selling 50 million phones a year. Back then, newspapers ached to have a digital offering, knowing their survival depended on multiplying content and platform alike.

Back then, smartphones did not outnumber humans on the planet by a ratio of 8:1, and back then the blush had most certainly not fallen from the Facebook rose. As recently as 2011 Mark Zuckerberg celebrated one billion people being on his social media platform with an apocryphal Facebook post saying it was 'just the beginning of connecting the whole world'. So what happened in ten years to make everyone suddenly so terrified of tech's magnifying and multiplying media capabilities? Well, in one way it is comment itself.

It is ten years since the publication of Clay Shirky's hugely influential book *Here Comes Everybody* celebrated the high watermark of faith in the internet's equalising abilities, where 'social sharing' was only good, only positive, only democratic. Commentators joined the tech-comms gold rush like everyone else and piled in. Not only was the public going to become a commentator but the commentators were going to converse with the public! It was all going to be great.

At first it was. Commentators reached vast new audiences on social media and their career stock rose as a result. They became their own publicists, tweeting links to their articles, engaging wittily and directly with their readers: comment became a feedback loop, a vehicle for social media virtue signalling and for a while all was well – very well.

Whilst commentators were enjoying dipping into the apparently innocent social sugar of the internet along with everyone else, they (along with everyone else) were noticing other trends around health, specifically mental health. It was common for columnists to write about depression and stress just as many commentators started to write about their own experience with Fitbits and digital tracking. But very good 'column fodder' was teenagers and tech. The *Telegraph*'s Allison Pearson wrote a famous piece in 2017 expressing anxiety that teenage identity was becoming hugely distorted by the narcissism of social media. She was absolutely right.

In 2017 my book *Fully Connected: Surviving & Thriving in an Age of Overload* was published. I named a new kind of health alongside physical and mental wellbeing: social health. What resonated most with readers, I found, and with my own followers on social media was what I call 'Techno Shabbat', a weekly digital day of rest. But herein lies the problem for commentators: digital consumers are nearly the only consumers left for newspapers. You can, like Hotel California, check out any time you want but you can never leave. In a decade of 'Here Comes Everybody', the commentsphere has fragmented into hundreds of millions of shards of feeds, shares, likes and retweets, posts and comments.

Comment itself is becoming devalued as a result. Everyone is commenting, social media is getting so nasty many are coming off it and there is something else, too: what is fake news but a kind of distorted comment? A wilful distortion of fact, spread in milliseconds is a devastating exploitation of weakness: the infatuation the media and consumers alike have had with their own opinions. Sharing comment became such a bull market it was bound to crash. Fake news is arguably its essential bear moment.

Commentators like Turner and Freedland are brave in some ways to address the shortcomings of the era, but the truth is this: if they bite the digital hands that feed them, this may be the end of journalism as we know it. And if they don't, they know that the social health crisis is only just beginning.

Money and freedom

Matt Peacock

Two years after the end of the Second World War, a small committee met for the first time in the village of Lake Success in New York State. It was chaired by the former US first lady, Eleanor Roosevelt, and the outcome of its discussions has since become the founding creed of modern inclusive liberalism: the Universal Declaration of Human Rights.

The committee members understood well that the poisonous messianic cults in Germany, Italy and Japan that brought the world to war had only flourished once the last voices willing to challenge racist martial ideologies had been silenced. The preamble to the declaration placed freedom of speech and belief at parity with freedom from fear and want 'as the highest aspiration of the common people'. The drafters were clear: seeking peace and prosperity while suppressing dissent would not lead to the better world that humanity craved.

The declaration is Eleanor Roosevelt's best-known contribution to the field of human rights. But it wasn't her first. Six years previously, as the US was consumed with its own ideological battle between isolationists resisting involvement in the European war and the interventionists (President Roosevelt included) who saw conflict with fascism as inevitable and necessary; she and her husband quietly willed into being a new organisation, Freedom House, dedicated to campaigning for democracy and civil freedom, with the first lady as its honorary co-chair.

Freedom House is now one of the world's most respected human rights NGOs. Every year, the organisation publishes a report analysing the extent of media freedom on a country-by-country basis. It is not comforting reading for those who remain optimistic that liberal democratic values still hold global appeal despite the rising tide of demagoguery on every continent. Today, only 13 per cent of the world's population lives in countries where journalists can report and comment freely without fearing for their lives or livelihoods. For 87 per cent of the global population in more than 130 countries, individuals and organisations with sufficient wealth and political influence are assured of complete immunity from any form of media scrutiny.

Strikingly, the majority of the 87 per cent are in countries ruled by democratically elected governments operating under the rule of law. A tyrant's death squads aren't the only way to silence irritant journalists. A multi-million-dollar advertising budget is an effective weapon, as is a media company shareholding linked to political interests. For example, for many years Indian journalists have told me (quietly and cautiously) the most extraordinary stories of criminal wrongdoing in Indian corporate life. These remain unpublishable (regardless of the evidence available) in the world's largest democracy as a consequence of commercial interests and political connections. A similar trend is beginning to emerge across Eastern Europe; in 2017, the country that recorded the largest year-on-year fall in the Freedom House ranking was Poland.

All of this matters greatly. Freedom of the media is at the apex of all human rights. Where journalism fails, corruption and the abuse of power soon flourish, leading to rising social instability and poverty as communities leach prosperity and kleptocrats amass obscene wealth unchallenged. All of this is acutely apparent to human rights activists, many of whom now seem to despair about the future of journalism.

So, what to do? Addressing the influence of corporate commercial interests would be a start. And in that area there may even be grounds for some cautious optimism. Here's why.

When a company makes an investment, it is placing a bet on the future. It has to generate sufficient returns to recover its costs and make a profit. For very large investments such as major infrastructure projects, it will need to do this every year, and for many years (even decades) to come. A country at risk of a rapid degradation in human rights (and, typically, the consequent impoverishment of its population) is a deeply unattractive investment proposition. Sinking billions of dollars into building a new factory complex in a country that five years later turns out to be far poorer, more violent and volatile than predicted can be an expensively stupid mistake.

All of which means that companies with large long-term investments should be strongly motivated to think hard about human rights risks, including focusing on threats to freedom of the media as the earliest harbingers of dangerous times ahead. Not all do so, of course. There are numerous examples of large businesses whose disregard for human rights (whether wilful or incompetent) ultimately leads to harm, public opprobrium – and a big hole in the balance sheet. But some companies do indeed think in this way, among them a number of the world's largest corporations.

Quality journalism needs quality funding, and advertising remains the dominant source of revenue for the vast majority of news organisations worldwide. Large businesses with big advertising budgets have enormous power over the financial health of the news industry. It is a power they must wield responsibly, as with any other human rights obligation, disdaining the repugnant tendency of companies (particularly in developing markets, in my experience) who relish that financial asymmetry as a means of suppressing all but the most flattering reporting. A nation's newsrooms are as deserving of protection from corporate contamination as any pristine wilderness, and once lost, are almost as difficult to replace.

When I worked for Vodafone (a major international advertiser, where my responsibilities included leading the company's global human rights programme), we implemented a policy that banned any employee or agency worldwide from using Vodafone's advertising spending as leverage to influence editorial opinion. Attempts to coerce reporters or editors by threatening the loss of advertising budget (or to secure favourable coverage by offering increased spending) were investigated under the same processes used in response to allegations of bribery involving public officials – a criminal offence under UK and US law.

Other global advertisers are also now conscious of the need to reinforce the firewall between newsroom and commercial department. Their stance is part principle, part self-interest. More progressive business leaders are increasingly worried about the prospect of political power unrestrained by effective, well-funded independent journalism, even in the most established and stable democracies. They also understand the social and economic context: it is not a coincidence that the Freedom House rankings bear a strong resemblance to global league tables for economic activity, investment flows and business confidence.

The best destinations for long-term corporate investment are countries where journalists vigorously exercise their freedom to trouble the powerful with awkward evidence and well-reasoned argument. As demagogues once again rise to high office, the best companies are beginning to realise that fundamental right is precious and under threat – and that they have a critical role to play in protecting it.

Why Meghan Markle shouldn't wear nude tights

Rachel Johnson

I'm embarrassed to think how long I've been writing columns for national newspapers – twenty years? – but at least it gives me a lofty vantage point to survey the peaks and troughs of the comment landscape and how it has changed.

I will leave to others observations as to how Brexit has turned readers into super-nerds and sucked out all the oxygen (editors report *mahoosive* digital spikes in activity on Brexity pieces – the finer details of Norway versus Canada are irresistible clickbait even to casual users of newspapers). Only identity politics and discussion surrounding trans rights come close to being as divisive and inflammatory.

Anyway, I've been in the game a while, and so: herewith my rudimentary thoughts. In the last twenty years, very few newbies have stormed the citadels of comment (hat tips to Marina Hyde, Camilla Long, Tanya Gold, Isabel Hardman, Clare Foges), which are mainly occupied by older white men writing about important matters of state, and – breaking news – the tabloids are stuck in the last century when it comes to gender.

If you're a man on *The Times* or *The Sunday Times*, the *Telegraph*, the *Guardian*, the *Observer*, you can write about anything you like because you have a penis. This means you can self-identify as an *homme sérieux*.

You can write about freedom of speech (David Aaronovitch's pet subject) or planning (Simon Jenkins) or civil liberties (Henry

49

Porter). I could go on, and I will. You can write about the history of Toryism (Matthew Parris), Brexit (Adam Boulton), green or anti-green crap (George Monbiot, Matthew Ridley) but if you don't have a pet subject, if you are a man, no problem. There's always politics, politics, politics.

The weeks Peter Hitchens isn't writing about – I mean against – the liberalisation of drugs or the liberalisation of marriage, he writes about politics. It is the safe default subject, and even better: politics never stops, it is a banker of a subject, week after week, year after year, decade after decade.

If you have a penis you will never have to flip through the *Daily Mail*, anxious, wondering, 'Mmm. Wonder if the *non-surgical nose job* will make the lead or a nib' – or whatever – as I did for six straight years at the *Mail on Sunday*.

Honourable exceptions should be noted: women on *The Times* and *Sunday Times* and *Guardian* and *Observer* – from Sarah Baxter to Polly Toynbee – are also allowed to write about politics (domestic and international) but not so much on the tabloids, where women (with honourable exceptions such as Dame Ann Leslie and... um, Dame Ann Leslie) are kept in the mummy track.

As a female columnist, you are laughed out of court if you pitch a column about Brexit or the environment or politics. In the end, you give up pitching them, because you know that you will hit a brick wall, but if you suggest writing an entire column on why-oh-why Meghan Markle shouldn't wear nude tights, the editor will bite your arm off.

You are then sucked into a vicious cycle. When Kate Middleton is pregnant again you start writing the 'Mum of three, dos and don'ts' column in your own head.

When a woman journalist starts writing for a tabloid, as night follows day, she has to tackle subjects – the Royals, celebrities, the appearance of celebrities, weight, the Beckhams, herself, her children – that no self-respecting man would touch with a bargepole. As Allegra Stratton's guest column for the *Mail on Sunday* on combining breastfeeding with covering the last election proved, women are expected to expose themselves in the papers in the way that male editors never demand of other men.

I've done my share of this in my time, and for good money and great editors – although after Liz Jones revealed she tried to steal her husband's sperm from a used condom in a bin in order to inseminate herself she helpfully killed off the female confessional column, as there was no way anyone could (or would) compete with that level of car-crash self-commentary (the only male who comes near this is the brilliant Giles Coren).

I do get why there has to be a contrast of male and female 'voices' in the book – but in my dreams, editors would mix it up a bit more than they have over my career. They would commission more counter-intuitively. I remember going to the planning conference at the *Mail on Sunday* for Prince Harry's wedding, and then lingering in my then editor's office afterwards. 'Why don't you get Liz Jones to write the leader, and Peter Hitchens to cover the clothes?' I suggested. Geordie scoffed, which is why he's now the all-powerful editor of the *Daily Mail*, more influential than most Cabinet ministers, and I'm currently kicking my heels on the back benches, but still.

I stand by my thought.

Sacred fact, profane data

Sanjay Nazerali

There's 200ml of water in this glass. Whether the glass is half-full or half-empty is now entirely up for grabs for commentators, depending on how optimistic they are. But there is consensus around the 200ml. The value of comment and opinion has always been to interpret facts, to find new ways of looking at them, and to open our minds to different ways of seeing the world. For comment to have this liberating power, we need to agree on fact. When we don't, comment has little utility beyond cheerleading and rabble-rousing.

The promise of the data revolution was like manna from heaven for commentators. Armed with irrefutable fact, we were in a position to comment on areas where we'd barely caught a glimpse of reality. Facebook could show us what people were really talking about, how many of them, where they lived, what they thought about climate change. Google Trends could offer us instant access to the world's concerns and tell us whether privacy really mattered. Clever geolocation could show us the migration of the Rohingyas.

News reporters, too, enjoyed the power of this technology. Data-driven technology predicted election outcomes more accurately than weary survey techniques. The *Guardian* was able to show, beyond any doubt, the type, location and casualties caused by 16,000 IED attacks in its Afghanistan War Logs.

As WikiLeaks showed us, holding power to account is much easier when technology enables us to scrape together every

Freedom of Information request at the touch of a button; when every citizen armed with a mobile phone is, essentially, a new source; when the truth is only a tweet or two away. Secrets were rapidly becoming a thing of the past.

For commentators, the rewards were richer still. Visualisation enabled us to comment on the rapidity of climate change with breathtaking power; Twitter feeds let our audience talk back to us at scale, creating a true dialogue; and page views showed us whether our audience was really engaging with us. We could even A/B test different headlines to see how our audience wanted to read a story, tweaking copy at the touch of a button.

The utopian vision was that comment would rise to power, helping people worldwide to understand, interpret and speak to each other around a single version of the truth. Together, we could make sense of an increasingly complex world. Then the bubble burst through a series of unintended consequences.

We've woken up to the fact that data is a valuable commodity, which is subject to theft and misuse. Industry makes a great deal of money by capturing and using people's data, but it didn't take much for that data to be transferred to Cambridge Analytica or, probably, any number of state-sponsored Russian data laboratories. This has, of course, escalated to the point of regulatory intervention, with the introduction of GDPR. Beyond crime, however, there are three 'design flaws' inherent in all data-led activity, from marketing to journalism to policy development.

Firstly, the algorithms that power data-led activity are necessarily driven by one thing: response. At the most simplistic level, I will only see things which the algorithm knows I like. While this kind of optimisation drives efficiency in business, it creates echo chambers in the public space. We inhabit ever-tighter social networks in which we only hear the opinions of those we agree with. These networks have become a breeding ground for 'alternative facts', destroying the ideal that data is able to create a single version of the truth. For comment and opinion, this is life-threatening: in the social space, we don't have a truth we agree on and we don't have the ability to influence people's perceptions.

The second 'design flaw' in digital data is that it is purely behavioural. We only see *what* people do, not *why* they do it. *Why* is the most powerful word in the commentator's lexicon. The facts are there; we seek to make sense of them by understanding *why* they have come to be, and what might result. Brexit is a useful case-in-point. Data told us who Brexiteers and Remainers are, but it has given us no insight into motivations. We could talk about class, but then we have Jacob Rees-Mogg. We could talk about the North, but then we have Kent. To get to motivations, we've had to do things the old-fashioned way: listen, understand and interpret. David Goodhart identified 'Somewheres' and 'Anywheres', not an algorithm.

The final 'design flaw' with data is that it does the opposite of comment by fixating on the short-term. Data is structured to please people right now. It'll give them the Amazon recommendations and Facebook stories they want right now. It isn't generally structured to think about what they might want or need in the longer-term. By contrast, commentators generally take a single piece of news and use it as a way of opening up a longer-term discussion. From a single story about pay, an entire social conversation around the gender pay gap arises. From a single murder, terms such as 'institutional racism' come into existence and continue to be debated twenty-five years later.

Data has not delivered on our ideal of a single version of the truth, which we can then interpret and help people to understand. We need to be careful about what we're asking the data to do for us. If we're fact-checking or scraping records, we're on pretty safe ground. If we're looking for the insight and human truths on which comment is based, it's dangerous to rely on data. It's back to what has always made us valuable: listening, interpreting and narrating.

A view from below

Solomon Elliott

While working as an English teacher in South London, I was unsettled by the return of inflammatory rhetoric creeping back into public debate. Newspapers were publishing stories suggesting the rise of multicultural Britain signalled its destruction, and that half of our nation's Muslim community would keep the identities of ISIS supporters hidden from the police. One commentator likened migrants to 'cockroaches'. This was just a few years ago.

I was even more concerned about the impact this bigotry was having on my pupils. How could I explain to Artur, an unaccompanied minor from Albania, or Mahmoud, a Syrian refugee, that to some in our country, they were just immigrants 'draining' the wealth of the public purse?

Everyone has the right to free speech, so I decided to create *The Student View* to give young people a chance to share their world through words. Launched in September 2016, *The Student View* is an online publication written by students, for students. My team and I are on a mission to create a newsroom in every school and ensure all young people become critical media consumers and creators.

Before our official launch, I piloted the idea during my second year on the Teach First programme. Our first intervention group was a sparky bunch of a majority of 11-to-12-year-old boys who were underperforming in English. A common remark from my pupils was: 'Nobody really cares what we think, so what's the point?' Their apathy was no surprise to me.

Commentland

A 2016 survey published by City University London reported that 94 per cent of the British journalism industry is white. In contrast, 26 per cent of England's schoolchildren come from an ethnic minority background. Our press needs a vibranium-charged jolt to reconfigure its current make-up and reflect the population it serves.

The project was initially met with resistance from some in the group. One claimed he was 'not good at writing' because he was in a 'low-ability' set. I rustled up a few teacher tricks to get the boys on side. One scheme involved giving pupils on the programme a pass to skip the lunch queue, much to the anger of their peers...

Once they came into my classroom, the cheeky chappies slurped spag bol, frantically typing to have their say. The chance to write about their favourite footballer, rather than mimicking him in the playground, was an experience 'way better than actual English lessons!'

As soon as they got the hang of it, they were hooked. One boy, who had scored the reading age of a seven-year-old at the start of the course, achieved the reading age of a 12-year-old by the end.

I invited friends teaching in schools across London to encourage their pupils to share stories, too. One girl from West London described the pain she felt on her way home from school when she was told: 'Go back to Syria, you don't belong here.' Another student told of his experiences as a special needs learner, luring the audience in with the clever headline 'Wahts it liek growing up wtih dislexia?'

Through publication, we empower our participants so they continue to speak out long after they finish the programme. Adam Abdullah, 15, has done just this. Reflecting on his time with us in 2017, he said *The Student View* allows pupils 'to genuinely communicate your ideas'. Adam continues to write in his spare time and recently wrote a piece about the causes of knife crime which he addressed to the UN's Special Rapporteur on extreme poverty and human rights. This powerful piece was published by *Vice UK* in November 2018.

To combat digital disruption, we reconnect journalists with young people in their local areas. The disconnection of journalists from ordinary people in the digital age is a democratic disaster which enables mass distrust of the press to persist. According to research conducted by the Pew Research Centre in 2017, only 32 per cent of British adults trust the news media. To date, we've assembled a community of 80 journalists who have signed up as volunteers from organisations including the *Telegraph*, the *Guardian* and the BBC. They act as mentors, offering verbal feedback to our contributors.

Pupils feel 'privileged' and 'inspired' to create content under the watchful eye of a leading journalist and our volunteers appreciate the chance to see life through the eyes of a child. When Georgie Frost, a BBC *5 Live* presenter, met one of our writers growing up in foster care, she remarked that she had been reminded of 'balance, of how we need to consider the impact of what we write on others' as well as 'how important it is that those who are affected have a voice to tell us their perspective'.

Despite these touching moments, our work is challenging. The young people we meet far too often do not know how to use a search engine effectively, save a Word document or transfer a file onto a USB stick. Promoting media literacy starts with basic introductions to essential tasks like these. With such weak computer literacy skills, how can we expect young people from Britain's poorest homes to survive in the age of misinformation?

The news habits of our writers are different to their parents, the majority of whom grew up in a pre–internet era. While the television is still 'first port of call' for news among adults according to Ofcom, the majority of our writers consume news online via social media platforms such as Snapchat Discover's news channels.

Growing up in a rapidly evolving news environment challenges us to give pupils the right tools to spot misinformation, understand their privacy rights and develop their storytelling skills. We describe comment, at its very best, as a tool to assist readers to make decisions about how best to lead their lives.

Navigating the noise of competing voices is harder now because social media has made everyone a commentator. Performative outrage has become an essential part of the identity of some commentators fighting for attention in this clickbait era. Ill-informed voices with an ability to play on our emotions using soundbites have risen often at the expense of 'grey', expert opinion. It is not uncommon that those who cry wolf at being silenced by the 'oppressive' force of political correctness often have the largest platforms to express such views.

Readers are confronted with a public discussion in which personality trumps facts. While this results in likes and shares on social media as well as shouting matches among pundits, our public discourse is worryingly shaped by a small cross-section of British society. Making democracy the loser.

In response to this struggle to be heard, young people, particularly from traditionally underrepresented backgrounds, have taken a DIY approach and built their own comment platforms. *Gal-dem*, an online and print magazine written exclusively by women and non-binary people of colour for all to read is one brilliant example.

Currently, potential talent is put off by the unappealing prospect of multiple unpaid internships necessary to be considered for paid roles. This unsurprisingly benefits those who can live for free with family and friends. The socially narrow recruitment pool is made up of informal professional networks that rely on nepotism and entrench social immobility further. Excellent work has been carried out by the Journalism Diversity Fund and Creative Access to attract talent from working-class and BAME backgrounds.

The exclusionary practice of working for free to 'get your foot in the door' must end to ensure entry to the journalism profession is fair. Otherwise, the media cannot credibly challenge the accusation that it is elitist.

Today, *The Student View* is scaling across the UK with the support of Google.org and the *Financial Times*. We hope that if the number of our volunteer journalists grow, we can reach more schools. Then, maybe by 2029, the nation's leading comment pages will have bylines bearing the names of our writers.

Sex and comment

Stephanie Theobald

Stories on sexuality that appeared in the mainstream media 10 years ago already seem positively quaint. There's a story in the *Guardian* about two Saudi Arabian doctors who want to change cultural attitudes to female genital mutilation by 'gathering evidence of its links to sexual dysfunction.' There's a piece in the *Telegraph* about how schools are seeing a 'worrying rise in sexual offences.' Ah sweet, you think. Wait until social media really kicks in and newspapers have daily field days about the evils of internet porn.

The year 2009 was also when my Australian friends Genevieve Murphy and Kate Barry launched their organic-tampons-by-post brand, 'Trinkets'. The hypoallergenic tampons packaged in boxes with cutting-edge designs soon hit stormy waters when beauty editors told Genevieve and Kate that they loved the product, but that they couldn't put them in their pages because of 'the nature of the product.' Genevieve harrumphed to me, 'It's not the nature of the product that freaks them out. It's the place where you put it.'

Yes, ladies and gentlemen… and others (because the transgender chestnut has also exploded since the innocent days of 2009)… we have come a long way with that 'place'. Vaginas and vulvas and clitorises have become, if not big business (although you can now buy vibrators in Sainsbury's), then definitely new feeding grounds for editors who realise that nothing sells better than a taboo. And frankly, there aren't that many of those left.

Hence the proliferation of some seriously savvy stories about sexuality, and specifically, female sexuality. Our new Kate Moss, Cara Delevingne, is openly bisexual, just as the new Beyoncé, Janelle Monáe, is unashamedly queer and sings about the joys of female sex organs in songs such as 'Pynk'. In the 1970s we had the so-called sexual revolution, but that was pretty male-focused. Nobody worried too much if women were having orgasms but, as society crumbles all around us, editors are starting to become a little more daring. And frankly, who wants to read another story about Viagra?

I never thought I'd see the day when the conservative *London Evening Standard* would start a campaign highlighting the ills of female genital mutilation. And when Emma Watson discovered the high-tech orgasm-teaching website OMGyes.com in 2016, her enthusiasm was broadcast around the world.

Some of this new female sexuality glasnost is down to a massive publishing phenomenon called *Fifty Shades of Grey*. Whatever you think of the book, published in 2011, it gave women permission to acknowledge that they were sexual beings. The plebs now know what 'vanilla sex' and 'safe words' mean, concepts previously only familiar to cutting-edge lesbians out on the scene in the early 1990s. And who'd have thought that a clumpy old word like 'polyamory' would have had such massive impact on the popular consciousness over the past two years? Yet editors are realising that hoary narratives such as lifelong fidelity have become boring to readers. These same readers have heard about polyamory from their internet-savvy kids and now they want to read watered-down versions for themselves in their daily newspaper.

'Gender fluidity' is another popular term and we're all becoming increasingly familiar with the 'transgender' word every morning over our cornflakes. Transgender is not about who your body is attracted to, it is about whether you identify as a 'he', a 'she' or a 'they'. For this reason, I don't personally find it as compelling a phenomenon as who you fancy and why, and the topic takes up a lot of space that could be given over to discussing simple human desire. But honest discussion of human sexuality is still a hard one for editors. They feel on safer ground with the anger often generated around the transgender issue.

Another reason for the explosion of comment on sex in recent years is down to more women in power demanding more for women. The Kinsey Institute recently published a study showing that only 65 per cent of heterosexual women 'usually or always' orgasm during sex compared to 95 per cent of men. Labour MP Jess Philips has been vocal on the matter of the 'orgasm gap' (another buzz word of our times) and has called for better sex education in schools.

Mainly, there's a growing feeling of exasperation in women. Put it down to the endless nasty sex stories around the likes of Weinstein, Kavanaugh and Cosby. Following in the footsteps of the female pioneers of the 1970s, we are seeing a new wave of 'sex-positive feminism', and a growing number of us are choosing to transform our anger into the more refreshing and rejuvenating arena of pleasure.

And the internet is not only a bad thing. It has helped disseminate a huge amount of useful sexual information for women. It has the power to call sexist companies out. Take the recent uproar, reported by the BBC, over the award-winning vibrator, Ose, which was withdrawn from the January 2019 CES electronics show in Las Vegas. CES is the largest show of its kind in the world and notoriously male-centric. Female-bodied sex robots and Amazon-supported 'virtual brothels' are welcome at the show but not, apparently, aids that might bring pleasure to women. But stories such as these slowly help put a stop to such casual sexism.

Check out also the proliferation of Instagram accounts, including @clubclitoris and @the.vulva.gallery or Scarlet Curtis's and Grace Campbell's Pink Protest which tries to dismantle the stigma attached to things such as female masturbation and periods. Today, the glossies are all over designer tampons and moon cups, a phenomenon formerly only known about by vegan feminist separatists residing in Brighton in the 1980s.

Meg Mathews was recently the special guest speaker at a champagne-fuelled evening in London thrown by Swedish high-end 'feminine care' brand Intimina. Mathews' thoughts on post-menopause sexuality on her platform www.megsmenopause.com have achieved the feat of eliciting almost as much media interest as her erstwhile bust-ups with former husband Noel Gallagher.

Unfortunately, sex stories still tend to focus on negative aspects of sexuality: rape, abuse, #metoo stuff. And I am bored of being told by editors that I can write about sex, as long as it's not too 'icky' (read: honest). But a recent positive development has been to place female sexuality in the 'wellness' category. This was first seen at Gwyneth Paltrow's pop-up Goop store in West London. Alongside the store's fancy cashmere jumpers and expensive make-up there was a 'sex cabinet' containing lubricants and vibrators and yoni eggs. Mainly, the cabinet was symbolic. It said: healthy sexuality is an integral part of female wellbeing and can no longer be ignored or seen as an indulgence.

We are also starting to see some real reporting on more tricky aspects of female heath, such as vulvodynia, a generalised term of pain of the vulva. Women have Mustangs to the penny-farthings of the male genitalia (in 2016 I reported in the *Guardian* that French socio-medical researcher Odile Fillod had created the world's first open-source, anatomically correct, printable 3D clitoris). And yet research on our complicated machinery still lags behind men. As I reveal in my book *Sex Drive: On the Road to a Pleasure Revolution*, while many female sexuality experts quote the figure of 8,000 nerve endings in a clitoris compared to 4,000 in a penis, this figure actually comes from research on a sheep's clitoris undertaken in the early 1990s.

Still, dealing with orgasms, feminism and body image now feels like an essential part of being a modern woman. This is why this area of reporting will continue to explode and gradually become more finessed.

The commentators' journey towards Brexit

Peter Morgan

Way back in the innocent Spring of 2016, champions of the Remain campaign were derided for orchestrating 'Project Fear'. Buccaneering Leavers urged us to shake off our European shackles and 52 per cent of us agreed we should. How ironic that the outcomes facing us as Brexit fast approaches seem more frightening by the day.

I suspect that, like you, I have read the commentary around Brexit with mounting trepidation. As the drama reaches a climax it is interesting to reflect how the argument has developed through the comment columns of results day. One year later and right now.

Since the bombshell dropped on the morning of 23 June 2016, arguments for and against Brexit have sharpened from the theoretical to the practical. An evolution well illustrated by the recent big surprise that it was a big surprise to Brexit Secretary Dominic Raab that a huge chunk of our imports arrive through the port of Dover and risk severe disruption (surely a prime contender for the 2018 'No Shit Sherlock?' awards).

According to the *Financial Times* the cabinet has been told, in the event of no deal the *best*-case scenario is that checks would reduce trade on the Calais–Dover route to 25 per cent of capacity, while plans are being drawn up to maintain supplies of food and medicine. Of course the commentators have focused on the essentials of life, but spare a thought for British industry. Take my old shop Rolls-Royce (where I enjoyed eight years as

Corporate Affairs Director). Rolls is Europe's biggest aircraft engine maker and one of the UK's main exporters. Each engine has around 18,000 components, many sourced from continental Europe. The absence of just one will halt the production line.

There is just one thing the commentators have agreed on since day one. History is being made for good or bad. On the morning of 24 June 2016 Philip Stephens intoned that a political establishment has been shattered by an insurgency against the elites. Over in the *Guardian*'s newsroom Jonathan Freedland opined that we had woken up in a different country.

Addressing the queasiness of the 48 per cent, Boris Johnson was on hand to reassure us that the verdict of history would be that we had got it right, leaving Richard Littlejohn in the *Mail* to put the boot in and rant that the Remain camp were always going to be sore losers.

Much ink was spilled in those early days over David Cameron's departure, the enormity of the referendum result and (interestingly) the possibility of a second referendum. Looking back I am struck how little reflection was given to the European perspective of Brexit, and by one other critical omission. Back in June 2016 you might have looked but you would not have found commentary pointing to the hazards presented by messing with the Northern Ireland border.

By the first anniversary of the referendum earthquake a significant aftershock was rocking the political landscape. Theresa May's cunning wheeze to exchange her party's 21-point poll advantage for a bigger majority in parliament and a stronger Brexit negotiating position had not gone exactly as planned. In Andrew Rawnsley's judgement Mrs May had been reduced to a 'zombie prime minister' while the other European leaders were concluding that Britain had finally taken leave of its senses.

In late June 2017, election fall-out dominated the commentary and the prime minister's obituaries were in final draft. Janan Ganesh in the *Financial Times* concluded Mrs May was just one scandal or misjudgement away from oblivion. Philip Stephens wrote that in truth Mrs May's premiership was over. Polly Toynbee was not alone in lamenting a government that would be kept in place only by the good will of the Democratic Unionist Party. Ignominy, she concluded, doesn't get much more mortifying than that. While across the political divide words appeared in print that would have seemed almost laughable on referendum day: Jeremy Corbyn now looks like a prime minister-in-waiting, wrote Matt Zarb-Cousin in the *Independent*.

As 2018 draws to a close the commentary has tracked from shock and awe at the enormity of our decision, through the politics of prime ministerial change and cabinet turmoil to the Deal or No Deal drama of the Brexit finale. Commentators have entrenched on each side of the argument, although writers from both banks of the great divide are using increasingly apocalyptic language about the consequences of no deal at all. The prospect of a second referendum looms larger.

This seismic debate has divided ministers, parliamentarians, commentators, friends and families. It is terrifying that this close to midnight the shape and even the possibility of a settlement acceptable to parliament and the people remains shrouded in doubt. The great deception which has been cruelly exposed is that securing a deal would be simple.

Why the UK media failed to see the crash was coming

Vicky Pryce

Neither economists nor journalists, with some notable and honourable exceptions, covered themselves with glory in the run-up and then the aftermath of the financial crisis of 2007/8. The rapid pace of globalisation and massive trade and international capital flows had made tracking developments rather difficult. The inter-connectivity of financial systems and the crucial importance of finance in furthering growth had not featured well enough in the models used by most economists. A handful of economists were sounding the alarm but the overall view in the market was that the rapid acceleration in lending and asset prices before the crisis was nothing to worry about as 'this time it was different'. The media had bought the story and complacency generally prevailed – with the exception of a handful of columnists such as Gillian Tett and Martin Wolf in the *Financial Times* and Alex Brummer in the *Daily Mail*.

Tightening monetary policy to curb price pressures after a longish period of growth or a shock such as was seen in the oil crises of 1973 and 1979 had generally been the way in which downturns had started in the past. But in the run-up to the latest financial crisis central banks had been lulled into thinking that they had somehow mastered the art of keeping growth and employment rising with little impact on inflation. Indeed, in the UK, Gordon Brown had proclaimed the end of boom and busts and Sir Charlie Bean, the then-chief economist of the Bank of

England (BoE), admitted that 'we thought we had that central banking business cracked'.

In truth, inflation stayed down due to globalisation and cheap Chinese imports. The asset price bubble fuelled by misconceived deregulation was not realised or understood. But what was missed, as economists Rogoff and Reinhart argued, was that 'periods of high international capital mobility have repeatedly produced international banking crises'. So have periods of great financial innovation.

The world media, including that in the UK, could be excused as the issues were complex and the workings of the financial system were far from transparent. Bill Emmott, former Editor of *The Economist*, argues that Wall Street bought the regulators and that journalists had by and large bought the stories told to them by regulators, central bankers, finance ministries and city operatives. In truth, the regulators themselves had little idea of what was going on. Often, neither did the boards of banks in awe of the financial engineering performed by clever and handsomely incentivised employees.

When the first signs appeared that something was wrong, Ben Bernanke, the Chairman of the Federal Reserve Bank in the US, was reassuring markets in May 2007 that 'the subprime crisis would be contained... and it would not spill over into the overall economy'. In the same month, Mervyn (now Lord) King, then-Governor of the BoE said: 'I don't think there's any reason for people to be unduly alarmed' and, as the storm gathered, was adamant that banks should not be rescued due to the risk of 'moral hazard'. The then-President of the European Central Bank, Jean-Claude Trichet, originally refused to print extra cash to help the struggling eurozone. And in 2011, believing the crisis was over, he raised rates twice – not noticing that by then the eurozone economy had fallen back into recession!

Business news had never featured that highly in the UK. Few UK-based media outlets had sufficient resources to cover international business and economic stories in depth, except for the likes of *The Economist* and the *Financial Times*. But that was slowly changing. There had been the welcome addition of the weekly *Financial News* in 1996. *City A.M.*, the dedicated financial freesheet, was launched in 2006. International news coverage from the late 1990s onwards benefited from the huge expansion of available digital channels and the rise of the internet and search platforms like Google. UK penetration of business news by the likes of Bloomberg, CNN and CNBC had increased considerably in the run-up to the crisis.

The BBC was a bit slow in this area. Peter Jay was made its first Economics Editor in the 1980s, but its first Business Editor, Jeff Randall, was only appointed in 2001. The crisis changed all this. Robert Peston, who had succeeded Jeff Randall as Business Editor in 2006, was granted rock star status for breaking the story about Northern Rock's liquidity difficulties in 2007. In fact, he was accused by the Treasury Select Committee (which also interviewed other leading financial journalists) of precipitating the bank's downfall through his reporting! A year later, he also unveiled that merger talks between HBOS and Lloyds TSB had been taking place, which also unsettled markets.

Since the financial crisis and the Brexit vote, interest in business and economics has risen. But the coverage in the press still confuses. Is quantitative easing (introduced aggressively in many Western economies to mitigate the impact of the crisis) good or bad? Is protectionism to be avoided at all costs? Were business journalists in traditionally eurosceptic papers complicit in not spreading the message that the EU has in fact been good for the UK? Are banks really so much better capitalised that they can survive major shocks, such as a bad Brexit, intact as the BoE argues? Or has the debate become too politicised to allow for proper interrogation and for the business stories to really break through? And do you have the duty to report even if the consequences may be dire?

Commentland

We have a greater supply of and also listen more to business news now. Business journalism has become much more questioning. But as we are once again sinking under vast quantities of debt, is our press really warning us enough of the next crisis which is certain to come? It's not clear.

Quicker, smarter but still out of touch

Stephanie Flanders

Economics commentary has become bigger, quicker and quite often smarter since 2008. It has struggled to be all three on a consistent basis, but then, so has the rest of the media. The bigger problem is that the basic toolkit for thinking about economics and business has barely changed at all. We should not be surprised that people are turning elsewhere for solutions.

Back in the dark ages, 2006, you could admit to 'not having the foggiest idea' about business and economics. When I was BBC Economics Editor so many people told me they 'loved' seeing me on the news, 'though of course I don't understand a word'.

That era ended when Lehman Brothers did. After that everyone wanted – needed – to know what a credit derivative swap was. You could explain what quantitative easing was on the ten o'clock news and people actually listened. Or at least they tried to.

It was a learning opportunity that the likes of author Michael Lewis and journalists such as Robert Peston, now at ITV, or Andrew Ross Sorkin, of the *New York Times*, seized with both hands. Collectively, economic and business commentators received a crash course – pun intended – in real-time reporting and speaking more directly to the audience via blogs, Twitter and the rest.

One reassuring lesson of this period is that quality will win out. *The Economist* is the outstanding example. Since 2008 it has increased its circulation by 8 per cent but raised revenues from circulation by nearly 100 per cent and developed an enormous social media presence. The *Financial Times* has also held its own.

Another reassuring lesson, which those two publications often demonstrate, is that speed can be an enemy of depth, but it doesn't have to be. We are all under pressure to write before we think. On big days, especially, it would be better – for reader and writer alike – to have more time to decide exactly what is happening and why it matters. But as Matthew Parris likes to say, 'diddums'.

The best commentators – Paul Krugman of the *NYT*, for example, Martin Wolf of the *FT*, or Bloomberg commentators with committed followings, such as Tyler Cowen or Noah Smith – get to choose their own definition of 'timeliness'. They can also choose their format. Martin Sandbu's lengthy and erudite 'Free Lunch' newsletter comes out daily and has at least 20,000 subscribers.

Speed isn't the problem facing economics and business journalists. Nor do they have to worry about the underlying business model for their work – or at least not nearly as much as journalists from other parts of the media. What should concern them, however, is the fact that the economic institutions and policies they are writing about still have broadly the same default settings – despite undergoing the worst crisis in nearly a century.

I saw some of the gaps in the traditional economic prescriptions first-hand in 2016 and 2017, chairing a Commission on Inclusive Growth sponsored by the 30 largest cities in the UK. My first evidence session took place in Sheffield. It had been an unemployment black spot through the 1980s and 1990s, but the local leadership had dedicated themselves to following the modern recipe for economic revival – with impressive results. At least on paper.

In 2016, 72 per cent per cent of Sheffield's population was employed – the highest since the 1960s – and the unemployment rate was around six per cent, less than half what it was in the early 1990s. But public services had been squeezed by fiscal austerity, and the poorest parts of the city still had most of the social problems they had when unemployment was three times higher. A few days before the hearing, 80 per cent of the wider Sheffield area had rejected the advice of leading local politicians and voted for Brexit.

At that first commission meeting, the chief executive of the city council, John Mothersole, was still in shock. 'For years we've gone along with a dominant economic narrative which said any growth was good growth. Now we're seeing the consequences.'

The dynamics of the Brexit vote were complicated. It surely wasn't determined by economics alone. The same is true of the election of Donald Trump. But one lesson from these populist upsets is that it's not just the quantity of growth and jobs that matters to voters today, it's also the quality. Immigration is another area where we now see a gaping divide between the standard economic advice and real-life politics. Trade, increasingly, is another.

Many economics and business commentators pay lip service to this disconnect between economics and politics. They have probably written many a column about it. But in their basic coverage and analysis it is still business as usual. The mindsets which are most often – and most easily – represented are those of city economists and centrist economic thinkers.

This is no surprise, perhaps, when many of the leading figures in British economic coverage are journalists and economists who cut their teeth in the 1980s and 1990s. Back then, understanding how economics worked, from a journalistic standpoint, meant understanding why markets and privately owned companies were generally best. Why everyone did better when central banks were independent, targeting inflation of two per cent. Why a job, any job, was the best answer to poverty – that, and a more integrated and open global economy.

We think we're questioning some of those assumptions now, just as voters are. But we're really not. Economists need to do a better job of thinking outside the old assumptions and so do economic commentators.

Interview with Yanis Varoufakis

Julia Hobsbawm

JH – So, Yanis, tell me: how do you consume commentary and opinion? Do you read on a tablet? Do you like holding newspapers in your hand?

YV – I love holding newspapers in my hand but I don't anymore because I travel a lot, so I wake up in the morning and I start reading the standard four, five newspapers that I read every morning on my phone.

JH – What are your standard four, five?

YV – Well, being a Marxist I have to start with the *Financial Times* and the *Wall Street Journal* because you need to understand–

JH – Know what the capitalists are up to!

YV – Absolutely. Then I go to the *Guardian*. After the *Guardian* I read a couple of continental European newspapers, a Greek one, an Italian or a German one. And then I look at some daily briefings I get from specialised sources like your intelligence, which are like a daily report on the eurozone. And then whatever else my office or my colleagues and comrades send me. So that means two hours of reading in the morning. I wish I could have it in paper form but I don't.

JH – But you do turn to the commentators rather than the news pages? I turn to the comment first.

YV – Well, it depends. The moment I see certain commentators have written a piece, I read it immediately before I read the news. I hardly ever read the news themselves, the first page. Unless there's been some catastrophe.

JH – Do you also listen and watch comment, podcasts, videos?

YV – I have my app with my podcasts and I have seven podcasts that I never miss. The one I always start my day with is my friend Philip Adams from ABC, the Australian Broadcasting Corporation, *Late Night Live*. He's a friend and a remarkable journalist and film-maker and all sorts. So he has guests and I understand more about the world listening to this than anything else. This is my pitch for *Late Night Live*, I listen to Philip Adams. But I listen to other podcasts as well, I like the new quiz show on Radio 4. That's for relaxation purposes.

JH – Do you think that audio and podcast has caught on because we are so busy and always on the move or because it's actually a fantastic format through which to convey comment?

YV – I think it's because it's a fantastic format along the lines of the wireless. For me the radio is the most spectacular medium. It's the one that I absolutely adore. It ignites the imagination and is much more vivid than television. And podcasts are a fantastic way to listen to the radio effectively.

JH – When you read a piece of comment do you feel that commentators understood more than news journalists or as news journalists – how did you feel about the way you were commented on when you were making front-page news?

YV – I was usually mad at commentators who clearly wrote stuff they didn't believe in only because it was the particular line at the time. You see, you have to remember that the six months that I spent in government were very toxic months. It was absolutely essential for the whole establishment to get rid of me because I was a great nuisance. I was the finance minister of the eurozone who said no to more money, more load. To them, that was unheard of, and there was a clear character assassination attempt. You could tell, because there were commentators who wilfully and knowingly distorted the facts, and there is nothing more maddening. I don't mind being criticised as an idiot, I don't mind having every tenet I ever believed in being rubbished and shredded to bits, but I do mind commentators knowingly misrepresenting facts. After Trump's election in 2016, there was all this talk about fake news, and the whole process of generating falsity and propaganda that Donald Trump, Steve Bannon and the alt-right have utilised through Breitbart. But it was the mainstream press that was adopting those strategies in 2015 and I experienced that firsthand.

JH – But you know that criticising the press is never a winner and when Jeremy Corbyn did it recently it ignited yet more opprobrium – do you think that the media genuinely doesn't understand that it has some failings?

YV – Julia you are talking to somebody who doesn't know what the words 'political cost' mean. I don't give a damn about political cost. I will always speak to you in the way I speak to everyone, from the heart. I'm not being paid enough to lie and I really don't care about the repercussions of what I say, as long as I believe in it. But allow me to say I've always taken the view that when I read something that to me is disgraceful I will say it's disgraceful and at the very same time I will defend freedom of the press with the last morsel of blood that I have left in my veins so I think that is what is absolutely essential. We must do what we would have done to ourselves. We should be very critical of the things we think are indispensable, like free press. We should be very critical of it then at the same time defend it to the hilt.

JH – Yeah I mean I agree completely as it happens – let's talk a tiny bit more about that and then I think we're done. You've pointed out that the concept of fake news can extend to fake commentary. Can you talk a bit about that in your own personal experience?

YV – Well yes. I'll give you an example. There is this financial economist (I'm not going to mention names) who writes in important outlets – standard, liberal establishment media – and he's a commentator like Martin Wolf is in the *Financial Times*. Now this particular person decided that in order to be devastatingly critical of me after I resigned my office in 2015, he would make the argument that I was the one that actually wrecked animal spirits in Greece among the business community. So what he did wilfully, he took data – PMI data – on businessmen's sentiment and distorted the axis and presented the collapse of business sentiment. He made it coincide with my tenure when in reality that was a year before and by the time I moved into the ministry, business sentiment was actually going up. But when you get data distorted and once you demonstrate that the data was distorted you get no response. Then you know there is something seriously rotten in this kingdom.

JH – So do we need curators to tell us which commentators to trust? Can we be trusted to find out for ourselves or do we also get manipulated by commentators? We are lured by their beautiful prose but maybe they're less accurate than others? What's the answer to this problem?

YV – Well the answer is to be constantly sceptical. In my previous life I was an academic and the whole point of being an academic is that you have to be structurally sceptical, never take anyone on their word – remember what it says on top of the Royal Society, 'on no one's word' – we should all be like that. Like scientists. Physicists, you go to a physicist and you say 'I have this theory that this is how the universe works' and they say 'Okay, I will assume that you're wrong, let's see if there's any chance that the assumption that you are wrong can be disproved in the labs'. That's how physics works. We should be like that as citizens. Everything – we should have an open mind but never be convinced of anything until we have exhausted a process of elimination of garbage.

JH – Do you think one of the reasons why Britain is so torn apart by Brexit is because we are not used to having competing opinions aired so frankly and so freely? Do you think that Britain has been taken by surprise at the need to comment to each other about what's happening with Brexit?

YV – No, I don't think so.

JH – Okay, what's happening?

YV – I think Britain is one of the countries that has a heightened sense of debate and a very strong tradition of public conversation. I think that this country was wrecked by Margaret Thatcher in the 1980s. It devastated whole communities, it poisoned the well of society. Then New Labour came with its embrace of the City of London and Mrs Thatcher's bubbles (the spivs, to put it less politely) and created a sense that politics cannot be trusted to change anything since the Labour Party was co-opted by the spiv culture, and a very large percentage of British society felt not just left behind but held back, discarded. They were being treated like cattle whose market value had collapsed and they were being effectively sidelined. And then there was one referendum in which an irrelevant question to all this was posed about the EU. Most people didn't care about the EU, they just wanted to rubbish the establishment that treated them like scum. Then once you get into that and a very important constitutional question like EU membership, it becomes the focal point of decades of accumulated discontent that has nothing to do with this issue, then it's very difficult to have a rational debate about this issue.

JH – But my question I have to ask you is – that's just an opinion, isn't it?

YV – Of course.

JH – What if you're, in fact, not right?

YV – Well this is the beauty of democracy. Democracy is a regime created by people who don't believe that they are right, who are full of doubt.

JH – But in a world of comment, we are selling certainty aren't we? You've just given a very certain statement almost as if it's fact.

YV – Yeah but why don't we all preface everything we say by saying, 'What I'm going to tell you may be completely wrong but this is what I believe,' and then accept the very principle of democracy, which is crowdfunding and crowdsourcing the truth? So let's all agree none of us are in possession of the truth but together through dialogue, through honest assessment of other people's views, facts, data and so on we can synthesise the truth together. None of us can do it on our own.

JH – That's good enough for me. Yanis Varoufakis, thank you.

YV – Thank you.

Contributor biographies

Yasmin Alibhai-Brown was exiled from her birthplace, Uganda, in 1972. She is an award-winning journalist, broadcaster, author and weekly columnist on the *i* newspaper. She is a national and international public speaker, a consultant on diversity and inclusion and trustee of various arts organisations. In 2002, Yasmin was appointed an MBE for services in journalism. Two years later, she returned the honour as a protest against the Iraq War. Yasmin is also a founding member of British Muslims for Secular Democracy. Her new polemic, *In Defence of Political Correctness*, has just been published.

Jane Andromache Brien grew up in North London and moved to New York in 1985 to attend Bard College, where she now works as Director of Alumnai/ae. Thirty years ago, after the unexpected death of her mother, she bought an old farmhouse in Staatsburg, NY, where she lives with her husband Stewart and their son Alberto.

Solomon Elliott is the founder of *The Student View*, a charitable online publication where his students and the students of his friends on the Teach First programme could share their world through words. This project became an education charity, which delivers journalism training to hundreds of secondary school children across London. TSV's mission is to create a newsroom in every school. The programme is co-delivered by leading journalists from over 20 UK media organisations. Solomon studied history at the University of Cambridge and was trained as a journalist by Goldsmiths University.

Stephanie Flanders is a seasoned economic commentator and policy practitioner with high-level experience of working in London, New York and Washington DC. Stephanie began her career in journalism as a leader writer and columnist at the *Financial Times* before leaving to become a speechwriter for the Clinton Administration officials Robert Rubin and Lawrence Summers. She left Washington in 2001 to become a correspondent at the *New York Times* and served as principal editor of the United Nations' 2002 Human Development Report. Stephanie became the BBC's Economics Editor in 2008, later working for JP Morgan and – since June 2017 – Bloomberg.

Stephen Fleming is a public relations, media, communications and reputation management professional with 30 years' experience across a wide variety of industry sectors. He is a former *Daily Mail* and *Times* journalist who now helps businesses and individuals throughout the world solve the most interesting of problems.

Claire Fox is the director of the Academy of Ideas, which she established as a public space where ideas can be contested without constraint. She convenes the yearly Battle of Ideas festival and initiated the Debating Matters Competition for sixth-formers. Claire is a panellist on BBC Radio 4's *The Moral Maze* and is frequently invited to comment on developments in culture, education, media and free speech issues on TV and radio programmes in the UK such as *Newsnight* and *Any Questions?* She is author of a book on free speech, recently republished as *I STILL Find That Offensive!*, and *No Strings Attached! Why arts funding should say no to instrumentalism*.

Contributor biographies

Ed Gillespie is Director and Co-Founder of Futerra Sustainability Communications, one of the first international communications consultancies to specialise solely in sustainable development and corporate social responsibility. Ed has driven the creative direction of Futerra's work since its foundation and has worked with a wide range of clients, including Barclays Bank, Eurostar, Defra and the BBC. He holds Masters degrees in both Marine Biology and Sustainable Development, and his career history has brought him from working as a marine biologist to, in the last 10 years, as a communications specialist.

Julia Hobsbawm OBE founded Editorial Intelligence in 2005 and The Comment Awards in 2009. She is Editor-at-Large for Arianna Huffington's well-being portal THRIVE Global, a columnist for *Strategy + Business* Magazine, and presenter of the podcast *The Human and the Machine*. A member of the board of the European Workforce Institute, her book *Fully Connected: Social Health in an Age of Overload* was shortlisted for both Business Book of the Year and Management Book of the Year.

Rachel Johnson is an editor, novelist and journalist. She has worked for the *Mail On Sunday* and as a panellist on the Sky News debate show *The Pledge*. She began her career in journalism as the first female graduate trainee at the *Financial Times*, in 1989, before moving to Washington DC to work as a freelancer in 1997. Rachel has written columns for a number of outlets, including the *Sunday Telegraph*, the *Evening Standard*, the *Spectator* and *The Sunday Times*. A member of the Conservative Party from 2008 to 2011, she joined the Liberal Democrats in the run-up to the 2017 general election because of the party's anti-Brexit stance.

Dylan Jones OBE is a journalist and author who has served as editor of *GQ* magazine since 1999. He has also worked as an editor for *i-D* magazine, *The Face*, *Arena*, the *Observer* and *The*

Sunday Times. He is a Trustee of the Hay Festival and a board member of the Norman Mailer Foundation. Dylan was awarded an OBE in 2013 for services to publishing. He has written 20 books, including the critically acclaimed *When Ziggy Played Guitar* and *From the Ground Up*, U2's celebration of their record-breaking 360° tour. Dylan was also a prominent supporter of the London Garden Bridge Project.

Deborah Mattinson is a writer with more than 25 years' experience of providing clients with research-based strategic advice. Before co-founding BritainThinks, she jointly ran the Chime Research and Engagement Division. Deborah was also pollster to Gordon Brown, first when he was chancellor of the Exchequer and later when he became prime minister.. One of Britain's leading commentators on public opinion, in 2010, she published *Talking to a Brick Wall,* the story of the New Labour years through the eyes of the voter. Deborah is also Chair of Young Women's Trust, a charity that supports and represents young women in Britain living on low pay or no pay.

Adrian Monck is on the managing board of the World Economic Forum. His role encompasses public engagement and foundations. From June 2005, he headed the Department of Journalism at London City University where he was also a professor and a member of the forum's first Global Agenda Council on Journalism. He worked as a journalist at CBS, ITN News at Ten and Five News. He is a published author, having co-authored a number of books. His views on the news business have appeared everywhere from the *New York Times* to Al Jazeera.

Peter Morgan is a business commentator and director. He was the Director, Corporate Affairs for Rolls-Royce with responsibility for the group's internal and external communications on a global basis. Peter was Group Director of Communications for BT.

Between 2001 and 2004 Peter worked for the Weber Shandwick PR Agency. He was Joint Managing Director of their UK Media practice. The first 20 years of Peter's career was spent in the BBC as a reporter and correspondent.

Sanjay Nazerali is Global Chief Strategy Officer, Dentsu Aegis Network. Sanjay works with account teams to collect, nurture and explore ideas that deliver outstanding business value. He also co-ordinates strategists around the world to deliver original, ground-breaking insight and strategy. Following an MBA at INSEAD, he was appointed Senior VP, Marketing, at MTV Europe. Sanjay then founded a Top 50 media insights agency, The Depot, before joining BBC News as Global Director of Marketing, Communications and Audiences. An unapologetic bleeding heart, Sanjay sits on a number of non-profit boards, including BBC Media Action

Matt Peacock is an international business adviser, lecturer and writer. He was a senior executive with some of the world's leading multinational companies including Vodafone, BG Group and Ofcom. Matt has worked with board and management teams in more than 40 countries. Prior to entering corporate life, he was a staff reporter with The World at One on BBC Radio.

Vicky Pryce was previously Senior Managing Director at FTI Consulting (2010–2013), Director General for Economics at the Department for Business, Innovation and Skills (BIS) (2002–2010) and Joint Head of the UK Government Economic Service. Before that she was Partner at London Economics and Partner and Chief Economist at KPMG after holding senior economic positions in banking and the oil sector. She also co-founded GoodCorporation, a company set up to promote corporate social responsibility and in 2010–11 became the first female Master for the Worshipful Company of Management Consultants in the City of London.

Justine Roberts is co-founder and CEO of Mumsnet, an online community of parents sharing advice, support and product recommendations. Over the years it has grown into the UK's busiest social network for parents, with 5 million visits a month and 25,000 posts to its forums a day. In May 2011 Mumsnet launched Gransnet, a website for the original baby boomer generation to discuss relationships, news, culture – and, not least, grandparenting. Before Mumsnet Justine wrote about football and cricket for the *Daily Telegraph* and *The Times* and before that she was an economist and strategist for SG Warburg.

Sir Anthony Seldon is a leading authority on contemporary British history and education and Vice-Chancellor of the University of Buckingham. He was formerly Master of Wellington College, one of the world's most famous independent schools. He is author or editor of over 40 books on contemporary history, politics and education and is the author on, and honorary historical advisor to, Downing Street.

Geraldine Sharpe-Newton is a senior communications advisor. She has worked at the heart of media relations and corporate communications for more than three decades. She has been head of communications for three of the world's major news organisations, CBS News in the US, ITN in the UK and CNN International. Geraldine was a longtime President of the Media Society, and now is a specialist business Mentor for The Prince's Trust, on the Advisory Board of the Global Thinkers Forum, an Associate for Editorial Intelligence and has been named as the Chairman of EI's Comment Awards.

Gisela Stuart is a British Labour Party politician who served as the Member of Parliament for Birmingham Edgbaston from 1997 until stepping down at the 2017 General Election. Born and raised in West Germany, she has lived in the UK since 1974. Stuart was Chair of the Vote Leave Campaign. Since September 2016, Stuart served as Chair of Vote Leave's successor organisation, Change Britain. In October 2018 she was appointed as Chair of Wilton Park, an executive agency of the UK Foreign Office dedicated to conflict resolution in international relations.

Stephanie Theobald is a British journalist, novelist, public speaker and broadcaster known for her playful and thoughtful work around sexuality and alternative feminism. She writes regularly for the *Guardian*, *The Sunday Times* and *Elle*. She is the author of four novels, including her latest work, *Sex Drive: On the Road to a Pleasure Revolution,* published in October 2018, which is about her road trip across the USA using self-pleasure to find her lost libido. It has been described by *The Sunday Times* as 'frank and funny'.

Yanis Varoufakis spent a year as a Fellow at the University of Cambridge in 1988. In 2000 he accepted the offer to become Professor of Economic Theory at the University of Athens. From 2004 to 2006, Varoufakis served as economic advisor to George Papandreou, then Leader of the Opposition. In 2012 Varoufakis became Economist-in-Residence at Valve Corporation. From 2013 to 2014 he taught at the Lyndon B. Johnson School of Public Affairs at the University of Texas at Austin as a visiting professor. On 25 January 2015, Varoufakis was appointed Finance Minister by Prime Minister Alexis Tsipras. Varoufakis resigned on 6 July 2015.

Comment Awards

Winners 2009–2018

David Aaronovitch, *The Times*
Riz Ahmed, the *Guardian*
Matthew d'Ancona, the *Sunday Telegraph* & *London Evening Standard*
Anjana Ahuja, freelance writer
David Allen Green, *New Statesman*
Mike Atherton, *The Times*
Philip Ball, writing for *Prospect Magazine*
Simon Barnes, *The Times*
Rafael Behr, the *Guardian*
Roger Bootle, the *Daily Telegraph*
Alex Brummer, *Daily Mail*
Stephen Bush, *New Statesman*, writing for *i*
Camilla Cavendish, *The Times*
Channel 4 News
Patrick Cockburn, the *Independent* and the *Independent on Sunday*
Coffee House, the *Spectator*
Marie Colvin, *The Sunday Times*
Comment is Free, the *Guardian* & the *Observer*
Ed Conway, *The Times*
Rachel Cooke, the *Observer*
Iain Dale, *Iain Dale's Diary*
Cory Doctorow, the *Guardian*
The Economist

Commentland

Financial Times
Daniel Finkelstein, *The Times*
FT Alphaville, *Financial Times*
Jonathan Freedland, the *Guardian*
Hadley Freeman, the *Guardian Weekend*
Alexander Fury, the *Independent*
gal-dem
Janan Ganesh, *Financial Times*
John Gapper, *Financial Times*
Liz Gerard, *SubScribe*
A.A. Gill, *The Sunday Times*
Ben Goldacre, the *Guardian*
Miranda Green, *Financial Times*
Tim Harford, *Financial Times*
Johann Hari, the *Independent*
Allister Heath, *City A.M.* & the *Daily Telegraph*
Andrew Hill, *Financial Times*
Christopher Hitchens, *Vanity Fair*
Dan Hodges, *Mail on Sunday*
Oliver Holt, *Mail on Sunday*
Sunny Hundal, www.liberalconspiracy.org & www.pickledpolitics.com
Will Hutton, the *Observer*
Marina Hyde, the *Guardian*
Independent Voices
Clive James, *Prospect Magazine*
Jeff Jarvis, the *Guardian*
Simon Jenkins, the *Guardian* & *London Evening Standard*
Anatole Kaletsky, *The Times*
Lucy Kellaway, *Financial Times*
Simon Kelner, the *Independent*
Roula Khalaf, *Financial Times*
India Knight, *The Sunday Times Magazine*
Simon Kuper, *Financial Times*

Dominic Lawson, *Daily Mail*, *The Sunday Times*
Mark Lawson, the *Guardian*
Sam Leith, *London Evening Standard*
Quentin Letts, *Daily Mail*
Jonathan Liew, the *Independent*
Richard Littlejohn, *Daily Mail*
Natasha Loder, *The Economist*
London Evening Standard
Londoner's Diary, *London Evening Standard*
Robin Lustig, *Lustig's Letter*
Kenan Malik, the *Observer*
Nesrine Malik, writing for the *Guardian*
George Monbiot, the *Guardian*
Tim Montgomerie, *The Times*
Oliver Moody, *The Times*
Caitlin Moran, *The Times*
Mumsnet
Fraser Nelson, the *Spectator*
Sarah O'Connor, *Financial Times*
Hannah Jane Parkinson, the *Guardian*
Matthew Parris, *The Times*
Tony Parsons, *GQ*
Allison Pearson, the *Daily Telegraph*
Laurie Penny, @PennyRed
Robert Peston, BBC
David Pilling, *Financial Times*
Peter Preston, the *Guardian* & the *Observer*
The Public
Libby Purves, MailOnline and *The Times*
Gideon Rachman, *Financial Times*
Nabila Ramdani, the *Independent on Sunday*
Andrew Rawnsley, the *Observer*
Melanie Reid, *The Times*
Hugo Rifkind, *The Times*

Commentland

Nick Robinson, BBC
Jenni Russell, *The Times*
Martin Samuel, *Daily Mail*
Sathnam Sanghera, *The Times*
Bintu Sannoh, the *Observer*
Matthew Scott, Barrister Blogger
The Secret Barrister
Michael Skapinker, *Financial Times*
David Smith, *The Sunday Times*
Andrew Sparrow, the *Guardian*
The Staggers, *New Statesman*
Irwin Stelzer, *The Sunday Times*
Janet Street-Porter, the *Independent on Sunday*
Andrew Sullivan, *The Sunday Times*
The Sun Says, the *Sun*
The Sunday Times
Matthew Syed, *The Times*
Gillian Tett, *Financial Times*
John Thornhill, *Financial Times*
The Times
Steven Toft (AKA Flip Chart Rick), *Flip Chart Fairy Tales*
Ann Treneman, *The Times*
Janice Turner, *The Times*
Tom Watson MP, @tom_watson
Peter Wilby, *New Statesman*
Martin Wolf, *Financial Times*
Michael Wolff, *GQ*
Mic Wright, brokenbottleboy.tumblr.com
Gary Younge, the *Guardian*